THE
WORKING PARENTS
HANDBOOK

*A practical guide
to the alternatives in
childcare*

A PARENTS AT WORK PUBLICATION

First published as the **Working Mothers Handbook**

© Working Mothers Association 1981

First published	June 1981
Second edition	May 1983
Third edition	December 1985
Reprinted	May 1986
Fourth edition	July 1987
Fifth edition	August 1988
Revised	June 1989
Revised	April 1990

This edition **Working Parents Handbook**
A **Parents At Work** publication
© Working Mothers Association 1991

Revised	July 1992
Revised	September 1993

77 Holloway Road, London N7 8JZ
071-700 5771

ISBN 0 9508792 8 2

Acknowledgements:
Our thanks to BhS for funding this edition, to writer Susan Kerr,
and to all the contributors who wrote about their personal
experiences.

CONTENTS

INTRODUCTION

No working parent should be without this handbook. It's a combination of years of accumulated experience and painstaking, dedicated research by parents who have had to balance the needs of a demanding family life with going to work.

This current edition is the most comprehensive guide yet to every aspect of childcare. Whether you need occasional help or full time support, this little book covers everything - from questions to ask prospective carers right through to treading the minefields of tax and National Insurance if you are employing a nanny.

The numbers of new mothers who return to work full or part time have more than doubled since the first edition of this book was published in 1981 yet the debate on working mothers rages as hot as ever. Some may still say that properly managing a family as well as holding down a career cannot be done. For single parents, or for many families where two incomes are a sheer financial necessity, it **has** to be done. In other families, working mothers who love their children and enjoy their jobs too, can bring irreplaceable happiness and balance to their home life. No-one is saying it's easy, but, whatever your circumstances, the ideal is to have a genuine choice - or at least to go for the best available option! I hope this handbook helps you do just that.

While mothers often face a difficult decision over whether or not to return to work, fathers, increasingly and for a variety of reasons, are taking as full a part in childcare as their partners. At the end of the book, as well as offering some useful insights into the way individual working mothers have coped with their own particular juggling acts, there are some revealing stories from fathers too - sometimes finding themselves regarded rather as oddities alongside all the women at the school gate or the daycare centre.

Whether you are a father or a mother, there are bound to be times when work and home responsibilities conflict. The 'At Work' chapter gives helpful guidance to ways employers can be encouraged to adopt a more 'family friendly' attitude to those with caring responsibilities. Some organisations now recognise that adopting flexible working hours and benefits that assist working parents can help them retain and recruit people with the skills and experience they need. Using the good example set by these forward-looking employers, the 'At Work' chapter shows you ways to bring about change in your organisation - good luck!

All the very best,

Sue Cook
Patron of the Working Mothers Association

WHO ARE WE?

Formed through the efforts of several local working mothers' support groups we were launced in 1985 as *The Working Mothers Association*. At the time, we felt that the specific needs of working parents with dependent children had received little public recognition and that a national body was needed to promote their interests. Much discussion went into our choice of name. 'Working' was used as convenient shorthand and not at all intended to imply that parents who stay at home to care for their children don't work! Calling ourselves an association of mothers - which is what the name stood for - accurately reflected our membership base.

Eight years on, there has been change. Where both parents share responsibility for childcare, fathers are now more actively involved in the choice of care arrangements. Though still very much in the minority, we welcome fathers who are joining the ranks of our membership. Reflecting this change, and our belief that equal opportunities should apply as much in the home as in the workplace, we have chosen as our focus for the nineties to promote family-friendly policies for all parents in the workplace under a new slogan "Parents At Work".

Our charitable aims, which have from the outset ultimately been concerned with the welfare of children of working parents, remain unchanged. These are:

- To provide information for parents on how to find the best care for their children.
- To help them choose the most suitable type of childcare for their own and their children's needs.
- To encourage the setting up of local support groups throughout the country - currently standing at over 150.
- To share support and advice on coping successfully with the demands of childrearing and employment.
- To provide information to policy and decision makers about the needs of working parents and their children.
- To establish 'good practice' guidelines for members employing childcare workers.
- To work with employers on improving conditions and facilities for working parents.

THE CHILDCARE OPTIONS

Here is a list of the childcare possibilities to consider. We provide further details on each option later. Also, see the At Work section for ideas on combining work and family.

If you work full-time

A member of your family
Obviously many - if not most - of your family worries will be solved if parents can share childcare, or if the child's grandparents or aunt/uncle can help you. Even if you are in this happy position you may find some of the ideas in this handbook useful.

A childminder
Someone who looks after your child usually with a few others - perhaps her own - in her own home. She should be registered by the local authority.

Day nurseries
Some are Council run, but pressure on places is such that only children of families in particularly difficult circumstances can usually be considered. There are also private nurseries which have to be registered with the local Social Services Department, which can provide you with a list. Some workplaces run nurseries and some will take outside children.

A mother's help
Someone who is not trained in childcare, but who will do housework, possibly cooking and shopping as well as look after your child. Like nannies, mother's helps can either live-in or come daily.

A nanny
Someone who may be trained, either holding the NNEB (National Nursery Examination Board) certificate or another childcare qualification, or untrained, and who will devote her time to your child. Nannies either live in your home or arrive each day as 'daily' nannies.

A shared nanny
By cooperating with another working mother you can 'share' a nanny between you, deciding on which home to use as a base.

Out of school schemes
Facilities for supervised play after school which may be run and funded by a department of the local authority or by volunteer groups. May be held in schools, community centres, playgrounds or the like. Some will collect your child from school while others leave children free to come and go. Similar schemes run during half-terms and holidays, or sometimes employers run them. There is also a growing number of private holiday camps.

If you work part-time

Any of the above may be available on a part-time basis, or you could consider:

Job-sharing/ Childcare sharing

By co-operating with another part-time worker you can take it in turn to care for both your children. Increasingly now it is possible to share your job with a partner so that you both divide your time between outside employment and childcare. Such schemes are being encouraged by the Department of Employment.

A creche

A part-time nursery, sometimes provided by employers and often attached to educational institutions. (Full-time workplace nurseries are sometimes called creches.)

Nanny sharing

Two or more part-time workers can share the services of a nanny or mother's help so that she divides her time between you. A part-timer could share some of the time of a full-time nanny.

An au pair

Au pairs are not supposed to work for more than five hours per day. Their work is governed by Home Office regulations. Strictly speaking, an au pair is an unmarried girl, without dependants, aged 17-27 who comes from a Western European country (including Cyprus, Malta and Turkey) to live as a member of your family and usually to learn English. The term 'au-pair' is sometimes more loosely applied to British girls looking for accommodation and part-time work.

More information on each of these options is provided in the section Childcare in Detail.

Parents' Rights: Informed Childcare Choices

The Children Act 1989 came into effect in October 1991. Under it, local authorities are required to keep a register of all carers for children up to age 8, be it an individual childminder or an organisation, offering full-day, part-day or out of school care.

Every local authority must also regularly review all local provisions and services - their own, private and voluntary - for under 8s. They have to publish a report on the review, which will include information on local child care services and a map locating them. This review and report must by law be updated at least once every three years. Authorities must make this information available to parents, employers, carers or anyone else interested.

Seeing this information would be a good place for parents to start when considering work and child care options. You should be able to find it through your local Social Services Department, library, health clinics, Citizens Advice Bureaux and similar places.

The Costs

Costs vary considerably around the country, and from neighbourhood to neighbourhood within one city, depending on the local economy and pay scales. Other factors affect costs, too, like funding (for a nursery or out of school scheme) or experience (for a nanny). Remember that the person who cares for your child deserves decent pay, rights and consideration. Also note that paying a lot doesn't guarantee the best childcare.

To give you some guidelines, here are costs gathered in 1991 by WMA from around the country, with comments below.

	Cost per Week £
Childminders	40-90
Nurseries	40-145
Daily nannies/helps	75-275
Live-in nannies/helps	43-229
Au pairs	30-40
Out of school schemes	0-35
Holiday camps	70-280

Childminders Remember that minders do have outgoings - extra food, perhaps special dietary needs for some children, play equipment and extra wear and tear on their homes. Your local authority under-8s team or local group of the National Childminding Association (address at back of book) will tell you what to expect to pay.

Childminders are usually prepared to look after children from 8.00am to 6.00pm; outside these hours, a higher hourly rate is suggested. If you use a childminder only part-time she should also be paid more per hour as she may be prevented from taking another full-time child.

Nurseries

Private Nurseries and all-day Nursery Schools: Fees vary enormously. Some are charities, or receive subsidies from charities or the local authority. Variable hours. Fees charged by nurseries will include your child's food.

Workplace Nurseries: will cost less than most private nurseries, depending on the employer's subsidy. Charges may be based on a sliding scale depending on your salary or circumstances (eg, single parent).

Local Authority Day Nurseries: Some provide free care in certain family circumstances while others may impose a means test to determine what you will be charged. Hours are usually 8 am to 6 pm five days a week.

Nannies/ Mother's helps

Nannies are usually qualified and will only take care of your children, while mother's helps don't have training, and will often help with general housework as well as childcare. Whichever you employ, experience will up the cost. If you are thinking of employing someone in your home consult the section on Tax and National Insurance on page 52. Most nannies command more than the basic lower earnings limit, which usually goes up every year, so you will have to pay the employer's part of NI (an extra cost you cannot deduct from her pay). You also have to do a bit of tax office paperwork.

Living-in: Works a 45-55 hour week (sometimes including babysitting, most often once a week). You also provide accommodation and all her meals.

Daily: Works probably 45 hours per week and is paid extra for babysitting. You provide her meals while she is 'on duty'.

Part-time Mother's helps

A local woman who comes in, say after school or a few days a week, might be considered more a babysitter/ironing lady than an employee (if you pay her less than the lower earnings limit), and so might be paid on an hourly basis. Local childminder fees and cleaning person rates would be a guideline.

Au pairs

Work no more than 30 hours a week, and likely to be studying part-time so you must tailor your childcare needs around her. Lives with you, so you provide her accommodation and meals as well, plus extra costs such as 'phone calls, heating, etc.

Out of School schemes

Whether out of school or holiday schemes, some local councils run them free for all, but increasingly they have to charge. Private schemes may be subsidised by charities or employers, or they may cost a lot. Where snacks are provided (and they should be), there is almost always some charge. Many schemes offer reductions for single parents, low income and more than one child in the scheme.

Holiday Camps Privately run, may be a day camp or residential camp. Costs vary depending on what's offered. A sailing activity week, for instance, would cost more than swimming and trampolining. If you send your child to a residential camp far from where you live there will be transport costs, too.

Start-up Costs Don't forget to allow for advertising or agency fees for nannies, mother's helps and au pairs.

Considerations

Alone or with others Do you want your child to have one-to-one care all day or to be with other children? It can be good, particularly for first or only children, to learn to share and be tolerant. Although small children may not play together, they do notice each other. This may help prepare them for brothers and sisters, and later for school. There is however, the chance that in being with others your child will pick up infections and be ill more often.

Continuity Continuity of care is especially important to young children and it makes sense not to confuse your child by changing too often. Childminders are usually settled in the area with family commit-ments and so may be able to look after your child right up to school age. Young living-in nannies, in our experience, tend to leave after about a year or so - but because you are providing their home as well as their job, they won't usually leave you without good notice. Daily nannies/mother's helps are more independent of you and this may or may not encourage them to stay longer. It is probably true that older nannies remain longer with one family. If you choose a day nursery, you will probably be able to provide continuity of place (though childcare facilities are vulnerable to closure by local au-thorities or employers in times of financial stringency), but there may be quite substantial staff turnover and this would be a point worth checking. Au pair girls often seem to leave early - perhaps because of home-sickness - but some stay with their host families for 9-12 months or longer. Regulations limit them to a maximum of two years.

The morning rush How good are you at getting up? Can you organise yourself and the children in the morning and take the child to the minder or nursery in all weathers? Obviously it is more convenient if your child is cared for either very near your home or at or near your place of work. This

11

is an important consideration if you are thinking of sharing a nanny with a friend; it's often difficult if you live even several roads apart.

Space in your House

Can you spare a room for living-in help? Do you mind losing some privacy? It may be like suddenly acquiring a teenage daughter, or it might add a friend to your household. It can help if you are able to provide separate washing and/or cooking facilities.

Shift workers

It is worth asking if there are any registered childminders in your area who are prepared to do weekend/evening hours or, try and find a mother's help/nanny who lives locally and who would live-in for a few nights a week - and then return home for the days when you are at home. Shift work and awkward hours are a particular problem for nurses who do not always have ready access to a creche or nursery. We can only suggest advertising in the local paper - it is very surprising how accommodating many carers can be - the hours may suit them very well. For working very early in the morning (i.e. before 8.00am) and late at night we would recommend higher rates of pay.

Illness - your child

If your child is more than very mildly ill, a nursery or childminder will not be able to take him or her, as other children might suffer.

Illness - of your child's carer

If a childminder is ill, she will usually be able to make some covering arrangements through the Social Services Department of the local authority. A nanny/mother's help/au pair may struggle to continue to work, but you will obviously need a contingency plan to cope with the times when your usual arrangements break down. Grandparents, other members of your family or friends may be able to help, or alternatively a nanny from an agency, which is the most expensive option.

Remember that sick children are emotionally vulnerable, so they will prefer to be cared for by someone they already know, preferably a parent. Find out what your workplace policy is on leave for family reasons (see page 60).

Evening and weekend babysitting

A living-in nanny is usually expected to babysit one or two evenings per week perhaps occasionally at weekends. A daily nanny may be willing to stay on into the evening for an hourly fee. A childminder may be prepared to keep your child late or even overnight once in a while, for an hourly fee, but usually if your child goes to a childminder or a nursery you will have to find babysitters elsewhere. You could consider joining a babysitting circle.

Holidays	Nannies, mother's helps and childminders will all have their annual holidays as well as the statutory days off which may well be extended at Christmas and Easter. Nurseries close down for statutory holidays too. Clearly it is most convenient if you can arrange your own holidays to coincide with these. If this is impossible, you will need to plan ahead for alternative cover as a sudden change could well be upsetting and confusing, especially to a younger child. if you go on holiday, a childminder will expect a 'retainer' of 50% of her usual fee. Nurseries may negotiate a rate to keep your child's place open during summer holidays and maternity leave.
The second and subsequent children	For many mothers a second pregnancy and period at home makes a natural break from previous childcare arrangements. On the other hand, those mothers who are able to retain a childminder/nanny/au pair during their maternity leave speak enthusiastically of the advantages of this arrangement. It allows them adequate rest during later pregnancy and time to prepare for the new baby. Even more usefully, after the birth it can ensure that the older child's interests and needs do not get pushed aside by the time-consuming demands of a tiny baby. Furthermore, continuity of care will not be lost for the older child and there will be a good chance of a smooth transition period when the mother does return to work. Do not underestimate how tired you feel after the second child - it really is much harder than having just one.
Vague fears and worries	Many parents are concerned that their child should receive adequate stimulation from their daytime carer. This will depend most on the personality of your carer and their rapport with your child - whether a trained or untrained nanny, childminder or nursery nurse is probably less relevant. It is worth remembering that you are likely to devote the hours you are with your child more exclusively to him or her than you would if you spent all your time together. (If you wanted, you could arrange with your child's carer to encourage your child to sleep well during the day so that you and your child have longer to play together in the evenings.)

CHILDCARE OPTIONS, COSTS AND CONSIDERATIONS - CHECKLIST

What childcare hours do you require, including commuting time?

Does your job allow for flexi-time, term-times off or other different work patterns?

What types of childcare would you prefer for your child?

What kind of childcare is available in your area?

What are the advantages and disadvantages of the available childcare?

Do you have room in your house for a live-in carer?

What are the regulations and formalities of available childcare?

What are the costs of childcare in your area?

Can you afford the childcare you would like on your salary?

CHILDCARE IN DETAIL

UNDER-5s

Childminders

The legal definition of a childminder is anyone who provides day care for other people's children in the environment of the childminder's home for payment or reward. Under The Children Act 1989, childminders have to be registered with their local social services department if they look after children up to the age of 8 years. The authority must keep this register and make the information available to anyone interested. Each local authority designs its own registration system, but basically anyone who applies to become a registered childminder has first to answer a few questions about him/herself and any person who resides in the house over the age of 16. (The questions cover health, and ascertain that the person is able to provide warm secure care and whether anyone in the household has been involved in cases of abuse to children or violence. This is a police check. A doctor's and other references may be required.) The childminder's home is inspected to check that premises are safe, warm, hygenic and all equipment is suitable. The whole process is thorough, but friendly, and helps to ensure good quality childcare.

The Children Act "Guidance and Regulations Volume 2: Family Support, Daycare and Educational Provision for Young Children" sets limits on the maximum number of children of certain ages one childminder may care for. Her own children have to be included in these numbers:

No more than three children under 5 years, and only one may be under a year old; or

No more than six children 5 - 7 years; or

No more than six children under 8 years, of whom no more than three are under the age of 5;

The local authority has the right to set a limit to the number of children over 8 years.

A childminder accepted for registration will be given a certificate and visited at least once a year by one of the local Social Services childcare team to check that the premises continue to be safe and suitable, the standards of care are acceptable and proper records are kept. The childminder has to keep records of each child's age, date of birth, parents' names, emergency telephone numbers, and information on health problems or medication. Childminders will be encouraged to take out full public liability insurance (some local authorities are making this compulsory). This may all sound daunting, but most of it is just good common sense and the under-8s team are supportive and helpful - they want more provision for children too! They will encourage each childminder to join the National Childminding Association (NCMA), and suggest contact with one of the many organised groups of childminders in their area.

Finding a minder To find a minder, contact the childminding department of your local Social Services, who will let you know of vacancies in your area for a child in the appropriate age group. You can also ask at the library, health clinic, leisure centre, etc for the register and report on childcare provisions required under The Children Act, but some authorities may be more efficient than others about this. You don't need to make contact very far in advance of your return to work as the availability of childminding vacancies varies at very short notice. Finding a place for a baby under one year can be more difficult than for older children partly because some minders prefer not to take on the extra work and responsibility involved.

Once you have the name of a minder, go and visit her and decide whether you feel she is suitable. See page 40 for a list of questions which you can use for the occasion. The Social Services Department should be able to supply you with alternatives names if you are not happy with their first suggestion. In some areas registered childminders are in very short supply and, if the council is unable to find you anyone suitable from its list, you could try to recruit your own, advertising in your local paper or on shop-window cards or by word-of-mouth - ask your health visitor, for example. Should you recruit your own childminder, new and not yet registered by the local authority, be aware that by law she must register and it is in your and your child's best interests to wait until she is. Allow time for this as new registrations can take several weeks to process. If she is registered already, she should be able to produce documentary evidence if you request it.

You could also contact the NCMA (address at back of book) who will put you in contact with a local group who may be able to help you. The NCMA also produce two leaflets which may be of interest: Looking for a Childminder and Childminding: It's A Proper Job. These are free with a sae.

Some advantages	● She is almost always a mother herself, so will be experienced in childcare.
	● You can tell a lot about her quality of care by seeing her home, the playthings she provides, and by meeting her own children.
	● Your child will be with others and will have plenty of company.
	● Your child gets used to another environment where he/she feels at home.
	● Most childminders are well rooted in the area by husband's work, school etc, so they may be able to care for your child for some time, perhaps all his/her pre-school years.
Some drawbacks	● You will have to take your child to the childminder's house before you can start your own journey to work. It's important she should live near you.
	● There is no built-in babysitting.
	● If your child is ill you will have to find alternative arrangements as the other children might suffer. (If the minder herself is ill, the Social Services Department will, wherever possible, arrange cover for her.)
	● As your child will be with others every day, there will be a higher chance of catching infections.

Please remember that childminders are working mothers too, they have every right to good rates of pay and conditions like the rest of us!

Nurseries

To find out about day nurseries, ask the Social Services Department of your local authority for a list, as all nurseries are registered with them. This includes council-run nurseries, workplace nurseries, community nurseries and private nurseries.

Day nurseries are governed by strict registration requirements relating to staffing levels, space, light, safety, access, etc. In addition, the Children Act suggests 'good practice guidelines' (see page 42) to protect the interests of children and their parents. Staff must have satisfactory training and there should be a minimum of one staff member to every three children under the age of two, one to every four aged 2-3 years and one to every eight 3-5 years.

Most full-time nurseries are open 8-6, 5 days a week. A few close for a couple of weeks in the summer but most of them are open all year round apart from Bank Holidays.

Advantages
- Usually open all year apart from Bank Holidays.
- Don't 'fall sick'.
- Provide good basic standard of care and are subject to Social Services inspections to ensure adequate facilities and safety standards.
- Provide the child with a rich social life and can help to establish early independence and confidence.
- Wide range of toys and facilities/activities.
- A mixed staff, providing a range of adults for the child to relate to instead of just one who may not always get on well with the child.
- Subsidised nurseries can be the least expensive form of child care.

Disadvantages
- Location may be inconvenient.
- If your child is ill you will have to keep him or her at home and arrange alternative child care.
- Can pick up more illnesses from the other children.
- An introverted child may not settle happily in a busy nursery environment.
- You are tied to the nursery opening times.
- Few places for under-2s because of the high staff ratios needed.
- No built-in babysitting.

Council Nurseries

These are run by the local authority Social Services Department and you apply through your Health Visitor or Social Services for a place in one. The cost varies from area to area (being free in some cases) on a sliding means-tested scale in others.

Places in Council Nurseries are much sought after and only go to people with a priority need such as families where a parent or child suffers from mental or physical ill health.

Workplace Nurseries

These can be on the premises where you work if you are employed by a large company or might be a college nursery if you are studying or working there. A few nurseries are adapted to the needs of staff on shift work, for example, in hospitals. Some workplace nurseries may also have provision for a few local children to use them too.

Some workplace nurseries may be based on their own premises with part of the running costs being shared by a number of employers. Again, nurseries such as these may consider 'outsiders' if they have any spare places to fill so it may be worth making enquiries even if your employer is not on such a scheme.

Workplace nurseries have the advantage of being near your work so that you can visit during the lunch hour or even breastfeed a young baby (though you should check the nursery policy about visits as they may be considered disruptive). On the other hand, check the position if you leave your job as you may well find you lose your nursery place and thus continuity of child care too.

Community Nurseries These exist to serve a local community such as a housing estate, for instance, and can be used by anyone in the catchment area rather than only priority cases. Community nurseries are usually set up through local initiatives and although they may be partly funded by government or local authority, they are run by a management committee which includes staff and parents. The management committee makes its own decisions about staffing and fees and is responsible for the administration of the nursery so parents get ample opportunity to become involved in the operation of their child's nursery.

Fees in community nurseries vary. Sometimes they are based on a percentage of your income so that those on a lower wage pay less, or they may have a fixed fee. Either way, fees tend to be kept as low as possible and are not usually more than you would expect to pay a childminder and often much less depending on your circumstances. Costs are kept low because of subsidies and because they are often housed in buildings that have been provided on low or free rent. Also, parents are expected to contribute their time to fundraising and administration of the nursery to keep costs down.

Private Nurseries Some private nurseries are run by charitable organisations but most are run as private businesses. Staff may be nursery nurses, teachers, nurses, playleaders or simply unqualified. It would be advisable to check the ratio of staff and their qualifications. Also find out what type of activities, equipment and outings are organised for the children.

Private nurseries vary in quality, with the most expensive not necessarily being the best. A few are subsidised in some way and these may prove to be the best of the less expensive private nurseries.

With any nursery, you will find it is usually difficult to get in as demand outstrips the number of places available. However, nurseries may be a good option for many parents and it is worth persevering as places become available at short notice. In the end it may boil down to a question of good timing.

Because of the extra high staff ratios for under-2s, it is particularly difficult to find places for babies, but it might be worth putting down your baby's name on the waiting list as quickly as possible.

When choosing a nursery remember to check:

- Times and dates open.

- Staff qualifications.

- Space and facilities.

- Types of food provided.

- Equipment provided and whether any outings are arranged.

- Outside play provision and programme of activities.

- Cost of the nursery place and any likely increases pending.

- Amount of parental involvement encouraged.

- Whether day-time visits are permissible (as in the case of a breastfed baby if you wish to be able to continue feeding).

- Does your child need to be prepared in any way (ie out of nappies, able to feed him/herself)?

Part-time Nursery Care

Local Education Authority Nursery Schools

These are for children 3-5 years and are a means of introducing children to school, with an emphasis on education through play. Most offer only half-day sessions of two and a half hours but some do offer a full-day of 9.30am - 3.30pm and may even have extended day provision for working parents. There is no charge although you may have to pay for care after 3.30pm in an extended day nursery.

Private Nursery Schools

Private schools (such as Montessori) run sessions for children of about two and a half upwards. Length of sessions varies with some being half-day and others providing a full school day. Private fees mean that this is an expensive form of care.

Extended-day Playgroups

This is a fairly new concept and provision is not wide-spread but it is an interesting model for the future, and one worth looking out for if you are lucky enough to live in the right area.

Children from the age of two and a half can be left with the playgroup staff (who have been on playgroup courses). The playgroups are open most of the year, closing perhaps for three weeks in the summer, with sessions of 5-8 hours including lunch. As they are an extension of the traditional playgroup session as organised by the Pre-school Playgroups Association, some children may only attend for a half-day and don't necessarily have working parents. Parents pay a playgroup sessional fee but some funding may come from the local authority or charitable trusts.

Nannies

Nannies and other carers who work in your own home are not governed by the same regulations as childminders or nurseries and other group care schemes. They will not need to be registered or checked out by Social Services (unless they care for children from more than two families). Because of this, choosing the right person for your child where the care will be carried out at home is especially important - the nanny will ultimately be your responsibility, both as carer and employee.

Training and qualifications

The range of training and expected duties coming under the generic heading of 'nanny' is wide. Indeed there really is no definition of the term - the word itself is derived from the child's affectionate way of addressing a nurse.

Most trained nannies have followed the NNEB (National Nursery Examination Board) course, which is a full-time two year course including two days per week practical work experience, usually in a maternity unit, a day nursery and/or school. These courses, and others organised by BTEC (Business and Technician Education Council), City and Guilds and NAMCW (National Association for Maternal and Child Welfare) are run by many further education colleges.

In addition, people looking for work as nannies may have other or additional qualifications such as the PPA (Pre-School Playgroups Association) foundation course or a teacher training. The NCVQ (National Council for Vocational Qualifications) now has the power to offer a 'kitemark' to qualifications in childcare which may be based on the childcarer's occupational competence rather than a specific form of study. On the other hand, nannies - or more likely mother's helps - may be without any formal training but with some relevant experience of looking after young children (perhaps being the oldest of a large family).

In our experience, the nanny's personality counts as much as her training. Although the training includes much which is very valuable - child development, safety and hygiene, the importance of play - many girls may still be inexperienced in looking after one or two children in the home, unsupervised. An untrained person with a mature approach, imagination and perhaps several small brothers and sisters may in fact be more confident, if less well qualified. However, if you are planning to work full-time and have a young baby, it is best to look for a nanny with proper training and experience or, if untrained, someone who can demonstrate some years of practical work with young children.

Some advantages

- She will have time to offer individual attention to your child.
- Your child remains in the home environment.
- You won't have to get your child up and out of the house to get to a minder or nursery - or repeat the procedure at the end of the day.
- Nannies - especially live-in ones can offer flexible work hours to fit around your own schedule.
- If you have more than one child, a nanny can cope with juggling activities for different ages - and may become more cost effective.

Some disadvantages

- To pay a nanny a fair wage will be very costly if you have only one child.
- You will have the wear and tear on your home - and extra daytime expenses including food, heating, 'phone bills.
- Nannies tend on average to stay only about a year and may not be able to offer long-term continuity of care.
- She may be working alone and unsupervised for long hours - you may object to having unknown visitors (other nannies, her boyfriend) in your home.
- You may need to supply her with a car.

Pay, hours and taxes

The cost of a nanny will vary according to her qualifications, age, experience, and what you expect her to do. A living-in nanny will receive less pay, but you will also have to provide her with accommodation and all her meals.

On top of this (unless you are paying less than the 'lower earnings limit') you must pay her National Insurance contributions and income tax (see page 52 for details). You will need to review pay from time to time to allow your nanny to cope with increases in the cost of living. Remember that sharing a nanny - which considerably reduces your outgoings - may be a good solution if these costs are more than you can afford. Pay has to be balanced against conditions of work. Many living-in nannies would rather have free time in the evenings and at weekends than higher pay.

Indirect costs & benefits

There will also be some hidden costs if your child is looked after in your house as the premises will be occupied all day. Your electricity and gas bills will be higher from the additional heating and cooking, your telephone bills are also likely to reflect day-time usage, while consumption of basic foodstuffs (milk, coffee, fruit juices, etc) will be increased. In addition, you will be providing two, perhaps three meals a day for the nanny, depending on her hours.

On the plus side, there will be someone around to receive deliveries, let meter-readers in - and you are probably less likely to be burgled!

Living-in or daily?
The choice is usually determined by the size of your house or flat, but there are other pros and cons. It is difficult to assess accurately the relative cost - you could let out your spare room to a lodger and use the income to pay for a daily nanny.

Living-in

Advantages

1. She becomes part of the family and the children accept this.

2. She may be available for babysitting at short notice.

3. She can often still cope even if mildly ill.

4. As she's in the house, you'll avoid punctuality problems.

5. She may leave less abruptly as you provide her residence.

Disadvantages

1. She could intrude on your privacy, and the children on hers.

2. She may deprive you of a spare room for friends.

3. You may be inconvenienced if she entertains noisily or if she uses the 'phone, bathroom or car to excess.

4. You may have to cope with her personal problems.

Daily

Advantages

1. You retain your privacy when she goes home.

2. You keep your spare room.

3. She may be more established in the area and therefore stay with you longer.

Disadvantages

1. There's always the chance she may be late in the morning.

2 If she is ill - even mildly - she may not come in to work at short notice.

3. No built-in babysitting.

4. She is not as tied to you as a living-in nanny and might leave for another job more readily.

Hours
Hours of work need to be clearly established from the outset to lessen the risk of exploiting your nanny just because she is in the

house. Most living-in and daily nannies expect to work set hours, and usually work five days a week, beginning in the morning half an hour before you go to work and going 'off duty' about half an hour after your return (This overlap is useful to enable you to get yourself sorted out and also for the two of you to discuss the child's day.) Some living-in nannies also work some weekends: one Saturday every month, for example. Living-in nannies expect to babysit as part of their job, but would probably rebel if you went out more than two or three times a week. Some will also babysit at weekends, but again usually on the basis of say, one weekend evening a month.

Holidays

You will need to plan how much holiday to offer your nanny. About four weeks paid holiday in addition to statutory holidays seems to be about average. Holidays can be offered at stipulated times of year, eg to fit in with academic holidays. The nanny should expect to take her main holiday to fit in with yours.

A room of her own

Living conditions for nannies vary considerably, but most expect a room of their own with a television. Some are used to a small flat in a basement or attic. It is advisable to agree right from the start whether your family and your nanny are to lead separate and, as far as possible, private lives outside her work hours or whether she will be part of the family. Will she eat with you, on her own, or with the children? Will she mix with you socially or run her own social life? What do you feel about boy-friends staying the night? Points like this need to be resolved before the nanny starts work with you or they can lead to misunderstanding and difficulties later on.

Duties

You should also sort out exactly what duties you expect your nanny to carry out beyond caring for your child - you may reasonably expect her to see to the child's meals and laundry but further household duties or shopping need to be negotiated. (See Conditions of Service page 45.)

Sharing a Nanny

This is a useful compromise solution with many of the advantages of employing your own nanny, but of course very much cheaper. You and another family share the cost of employing the nanny and reach an agreement about exactly how and where the care will take place. The arrangement usually involves a daily nanny, but there is no reason why it shouldn't work with a living-in nanny who could, for example, live with one family and take those children to the other house during the day.

Benefits	Although there are substantial benefits all round, there are many points to consider before entering into this arrangement. On the plus side, the nanny earns a higher income than either family could perhaps afford as a single employer. Many nannies prefer to look after more than one child at a time, especially once they've gained confidence and experience. The children also benefit from - and enjoy - growing up closely with other small children, and form lasting attachments even when the share has ended. It can also prepare the first-born child for a new baby brother or sister, whilst providing an only child with the nearest thing to a sibling.
Drawbacks	The drawbacks are, of course, that arrangements can become complicated, and all parties must be prepared to compromise around a fairly regular pattern. Your child receives less than individual attention, probably in inverse proportion to his or her age especially if a young baby is involved in the share. On the other hand, the young baby must fit in with the schedules imposed by schools and playgroups. You will probably have additional expenses in equipment, eg double-buggy. Your nanny is more restricted in her activities and expeditions and may become housebound. Holiday planning becomes multi-dimensional, involving your work colleagues, your nanny's boyfriend and his work, and your sharer and her work, husband, and so on.
Other points to consider	Which house will the children be in? You could alternate for 'fairness' - remember that the house will need to be heated all day in the winter and that there will be additional consumption of basic foodstuffs (milk, coffee, biscuits) in addition to cooking meals. The wear and tear and general untidiness with older children can be considerable, while babies' equipment (sterilisers, nappy buckets, changing mats, prams, foodstuffs) require disproportionate space. You may prefer each child to have some time in his or her own home or you could decide on a small compensation to the mother in whose house the share takes place.

What are the ages of the children? Think carefully about how nanny will cope with the feeding schedules of babies and journeys to and from playgroups/schools in all weathers.

If household duties and shopping are to be part of her work, think how this will apply to each family. Will all the nappy and clothes washing be dealt with together in one house?

What equipment will you need to move? You may need a second cot and high chair (perhaps folding ones). You will probably need a double buggy, or a double pram, or a pram with a toddler seat. If a lot of equipment is involved, it may be easier to look after the children in one house.

Do you and your sharing family share ideas on how the care is to be given? How do you feel about potty training? About diet? Will this involve the nanny cooking several meals at once? Do you want your child to go out every day? Or go to playgroup? What would you or she do if one child bullies or dominates the other for any length of time?

Do you have contingency plans if the nanny is ill - it may be more difficult to find care at short notice for several children. Presumably the nanny will continue to look after an ill child, but how would you feel if the other child has been in contact with a contagious disease?

What will you do about holidays? Are both families prepared to take holidays at the same time as the nanny? You will probably have to plan well ahead.

What do you intend to do if either family adds a new baby to the set-up? This may be the time to stop sharing the nanny; which family 'gets' her and what will the other family do? Remember that small babies need a lot of attention and this one may have to compete with two toddlers (rather than just his/her brother/sister).

If you intend your child to go to a particular nursery school/primary school, how will this fit in with the other family's intentions? This is particularly important if you do not live near each other.

Finding a sharer To find someone to share a nanny can be quite difficult. Try asking friends, neighbours, your health visitor or friendly local shops for suggestions and possible sharers. There are several commercial agencies now which specialise in trying to match up compatible families. The agencies will also look for your nanny and the two families share the fee for this part of the service. The agencies usually charge a set fee per 6 months for keeping you on their lists. Agencies advertise in The Lady and are usually listed in local Yellow Pages.

Another way of finding a family to share a nanny is by advertising in your local National Childbirth Trust (NCT) newsletter. Many Working Mothers Association groups have set up their own local register on an informal basis.

Registering A nanny who looks after children from more than two sets of parents must by law be registered with the local Social Services Department, as are childminders (see Childminders, page 15).

Making it work   It may not seem important at the beginning, but it can be vital that the two families get on with each other. It makes it much easier to sort out problems if you like the other parents and generally agree with them, not only on childcare but on general matters too. Make sure you discuss at the start how each family will finish the arrangement if necessary (eg if they have another baby, or the child doesn't seem happy, or a better alternative comes up). Try and fix regular joint meetings, say every three months, with or without the nanny present, to air any grievances before these build up. Decide, too, which of you will be responsible for paying her tax and National Insurance and keeping the relevant documentation.

Finally, if you decide to appoint your nanny first, and then look for a sharer, examine your finances carefully, in case you have to carry the whole cost for an extended period.

Au Pairs

The term 'au pair' is applied to many types of domestic worker. Most people understand it to mean a foreign girl who has come here to help with childcare and to learn English. Au pairs from EEC countries have no restrictions on coming here to work. The same is true of British au pairs (for example school leavers waiting to go to college). Au pairs from outside the EEC should still come from Western Europe. They are covered by the Home Office regulations (address at back of book) which specify that they should not work more than 5 hours a day Monday to Saturday on average. Most au pairs stay between 6 and 12 months and many are filling in a year between school and college.

It is important to realise that an au pair is usually a teenager of 17 or so who is unlikely to have any training in childcare, therefore it is not appropriate to give her sole charge of a young baby. Also, because she is not likely to stay for more than 6 - 12 months, she cannot offer the stability of a more long-term carer. But if you work from home or have a nearby part-time job, or can combine a part-time place at a nursery or childminder with an au pair she can be very useful with a young child, and she can do some light housework and one or two night's babysitting. Au pairs are most suitable for school-age children, dropping them off and collecting them and supervising them for the two or three hours until you get home from work.

An au pair lives-in and this carries with it all the indirect costs and benefits and advantages and disadvantages covered in the section on Nannies. She should have her own bedroom and you should be prepared to accept her as a member of the family (au pair means 'as a peer'). You should also arrange for her to attend 'English as a Foreign Language' (EFL) classes, if appropriate, which are run by local authority institutes, Colleges of Further Education and private language schools. The British Council publish a list of the latter (address at back of book), and your local library should help you find public courses. Au pairs should be given some 'pocket money' - usually £35 a week or more. An au pair plus works longer hours and is paid more.

Duties

Remember that your au pair may be very unsophisticated and away from home for the first time, needing guidance and reassurance. You should make clear before she arrives what duties she is expected to perform in the way of housework, as she may come from a background where girls like herself never do such work! See the comments on hours, holidays, duties and her room in the Nannies section; it's all quite similar, except you have her for only 30 hours a week, she is less experienced, and you have personal responsibility for her. It is probably best to treat the relationship as if she were a distant cousin come to help you out for a year. Spell out duties clearly and professionally, but be flexible, too. Remember she is not doing this as a career; she's here to have fun and free time and learn about this country. Try to find other au pairs and British girls for her to befriend, so she can have a social life outside the family.

Finding an au pair

Sources for au pairs are agencies (look in the 'phone book) and advertising (perhaps with the help of an au pair or other national in this country to guide you). Very often you hire the au pair without meeting her because she is still in her home country. An agency may have details or you may exchange letters and photos via an agency or advertisement. A telephone call may feel a bit awkward, but it is a good idea, if only to find out how good her English is. Try to determine if she has a good sense of humour, and inquire about childcare experience. An older sister in a large family is a good bet: used to children and to helping in the house.

You will usually have to meet your au pair at the bus station/train station/airport. Hold up a sign with her name on it so she can find you. Once at home gradually tell her about local shops, leisure facilities, transport, places of interest, as well as training her in the ways of your children and household. Provide her with a bicycle, if you can.

If you are worried about the language barrier between the au pair and your child, make sure she speaks and understands adequate English. Older children learning languages at school may benefit from having a native speaker of, say, French or German in the family.

There are, of course, horror stories and jokes about au pairs, but many au pairs make lasting friendships with their employers.

SCHOOL AGE

ORGANISED PROVISION

There are many different kinds of out of school and holiday schemes which provide varying degrees of child 'care' for the 5-12 year age range. The names given to different types of schemes are often confusing and may give a misleading impression of their suitability for working parents. For example the local 'playcentre' may provide full child care or it may be just a drop in centre where the children can come and go as they please. Similarly some 'adventure playgrounds' will take responsibility for the children although this is not the general rule.

Despite the confusion about names, there are four basic kinds of schemes which are of greater or lesser use to working parents. These are discussed below, but because there are no hard and fast rules, the best advice is to visit your local ones and see if the kind of service they provide will meet the needs of you and your children.

Out of School or 'Latchkey' Schemes
These are schemes that are specifically designed to cater for the needs of working parents. They are typically open from 3.30pm to 6.00pm in term-time and all day during holidays. The children are registered on arrival at the group and will be looked after until collected by a parent or other designated adult.

Local practice will vary but a good scheme will collect the children from school, provide them with a snack and something to drink and ensure that they are happily occupied until the end of the session. Out of school schemes may operate in school buildings, community centres, village halls or purpose built centres. They can be funded and managed in a wide variety of ways, eg education, social services or recreation departments of local authorities, by voluntary groups such as Gingerbread or, run independently by parent-users or as a private enterprise. Charges will vary from area to area but many charge only a nominal fee to cover the cost of food and outgoings. Some schemes may give priority to single parents.

This kind of provision is obviously the best suited to meet the needs of working parents and a good scheme should provide your children with a safe, welcoming and enjoyable experience while you are able to work with greater peace of mind. Unfortunately, there are very few such schemes in existence and there are many areas of the country which have no out of school schemes at all so you may have to consider the other, less suitable alternatives.

Advantages of out of school schemes

- Offer a reliable form of care, catering for after school hours, half-term and holidays.
- Usually subsidised in some way so may be reasonably priced.
- Gives your child the opportunity of mixing with children of different ages in an informal atmosphere.
- Will provide stimulating activities and play opportunities in a safe, caring environment.

Some disadvantages

- You are tied to the scheme's opening times.
- Location may be inconvenient.
- A young child may find it tiring at the end of the school day.
- An introverted child may feel overwhelmed in a lively group.
- A school-based scheme may not able able to offer a warm, homely environment.

Playcentres

Most playcentres are funded by the local education authority and are run as a 'play' facility rather than as in loco parentis 'care'. They do not normally provide organised collection from schools and refreshments are likely to be limited to a drink and a biscuit. Staff ratios tend to be lower than in after school schemes and they are not always open every day of the week. Charges, if any, tend to be on a sessional basis.

Adventure Playgrounds

These grew out of the 1960s vogue for 'free play' and allowing children to do their own thing. Originally they were little more than patches of rough ground with a few large structures for children to climb on. Gradually over the years they have changed and now a typical adventure playground will have good indoor play space as well as an outside play area with well supervised activities. Many also provide a snack for the children and are open after school and throughout the school holidays.

As with playcentres the children are usually free to come and go but more and more adventure playgrounds are beginning to recognise the need for a child care element; so again it would be worthwhile talking to the workers at your local adventure playground. In general they tend to be more suitable for the over-9s.

Holiday Play Schemes	Many areas of the country have holiday playschemes which may be run by the local authority or by local voluntary groups. These may serve as a stop-gap for the school holidays but will not solve the after-school problem. The length of schemes varies from one week during the summer, to schemes that are open throughout the summer, Christmas, Easter, and half-term holidays. You will also find that some playschemes close for an hour at lunch-time when your child would have no adult supervision. A few do register children and undertake to look after them but this tends to be the exception.
Holiday Camps	Privately run residential and day camps usually based in large schools or colleges which are empty during the summer. They offer a wide variety of activities: canoeing, snooker, drama, filming, treasure hunts, abseiling, etc. Most are suitable for children aged 7 and up, but there are some for children as young as 3 years. Some day camps collect children daily from pre-arranged pick-up points. Day camps can be a useful try-out for a longer stay at a residential camp.
Finding out of school provision	The Children Act requires local authorities to register all organised care for children up to the age of 8 so it should be easy for you to find out about out of school provision in your area, if there is any. All schemes must be registered, whoever runs them - recreation department, education authority, employers, Social Services, private organisations or volunteer groups. Contact your local Social Services Department for the register. The Children Act also requires local authorities to review all childcare services regularly and to publish a report on their findings. In time you should be able to ask for this report to help you identify services in your area. The report should be available through places like the library, health clinics, leisure centres, schools, etc.

According to The Children Act there should be one staff member to every 8 children under the age of 8, and enough space and staff to ensure that 5 - 7 year-olds are not overwhelmed by older children. The organisation has to keep records on staff, of course, and also on each child, but just name and address of children is sufficient. Just as for school, you should be asked to sign a parental consent form for any outings your child goes on.

If you do not find any organised out of school provision in your area then you can contact Kids' Clubs Network (address at back). This organisation was formed in 1981 to help develop after school and holiday provision for 'latchkey' and other children. It supports local authority schemes and encourages community-based out of school schemes to be set up by offering advice, information, publications and research. It also has quite extensive regional records of out of school schemes and should at the very least be able to put you in touch with someone who can help you in your local town hall.

If there is absolutely no provision in your area then you may begin to think about how to join with other parents to start a scheme or how to encourage your local authority to do so. The Kids' Clubs Network can also help with this kind of advice and have produced two booklets that will help:

Up, Up and Away - a practical guide to setting up and running a locally based out of school scheme. It consists of ten leaflets on subjects from Getting Started and Staying Legal to Finding the Money and Lone Parents.

Guidelines of Good Practice for Out of School Care Schemes - recommended by the Department of Health in its guidance to The Children Act 1989.

For private holiday residential and day camps you should send for the brochures of individual organisations. A consumer's guide which lists and describes nearly 100 camps is available from The British Activity Holiday Association (address at back of book). As with any other childcare, check on staff qualifications and ratio. Facilities for under-8s should be registered with local authorities.

Individual arrangements for school-age children

Individual arrangements can be fitted in around existing childcare arrangements for pre-school children, or be worked out by using one or more of the following:

Childminders
Many childminders take on school-age children in addition to under-5s, including collecting them from school. One childminder is allowed to care for up to six 5 - 7s. If she mixes in younger children she can take a total of six, but no more than three can be under age 5. The local authority has the right to set a limit to the number of chldren over 8 years. Her own children count in these figures. Childminders must be registered with Social Services. See Childminders, page 15, for additional details.

Part-time mother's helps
The ideal might be someone local from the neighbourhood, often an older woman, whom you pay to collect your child or children from school, take to your home, give them a snack or their 5 or 6 o'clock meal. She might even be willing to do your ironing! And she may be

able to help fill the gap during half-terms and holidays. You might find such a treasure through ads in local newspapers, shop windows or by leafleting neighbours. As she comes into your home, like a nanny, she need not be registered with Social Services (unless she cares for children from more than two sets of parents). It is essential to check references. See Finding Your Carer and Interviewing, page 36.

Au pairs
If you are able to have someone live-in you could employ an au pair. See Au pairs, page 27. In fact these girls (sometimes boys) are generally better for school-age children than for under-5s. You could juggle her hours a bit so that she is available full-time during holidays. You could perhaps share her with another mother in a similar position to yours.

Piggy-back nanny
If you know someone who is still employing a full-time nanny/mother's help, she might be willing to let you pay the nanny to look after your children in out of school time. If she cares for children from more than two sets of parents she must register with Social Services. See Sharing a nanny, page 24.

School-friends' parents
If you work less than a full week you could come to a reciprocal arrangement with a school-mate's parent, each of you collecting and taking care of the children on specific days. If you work full-time perhaps you could pay her for looking after your child. If you pay, and she has your child to her home for more than two hours a day this makes her a childminder, so she must register with Social Services. See Childminders, page 15.

Consortium of part-time or job-share mothers
Some mothers have successfully managed to set up a 'consortium' of three or four women each of whom works less than a full week so that one is always available for cover. The children's schools are then given the emergency phone number rota and a sick child collected by the 'free' mother. Ideally such a consortium should include mothers who don't work in the school holidays (ie teachers!).

Younger sibling's daycare
In some day-care centres or company nurseries for pre-school children, older siblings are also allowed to be cared for on the premises out of school hours. This is more common in centres run by charities.

THE CHILDREN ACT 1989 - How it applies to parents and carers

All organisations or childminders, as well as play- and out of school schemes, who care for children up to age 8 must register with their local authority. Also, anyone who cares for children of more than two sets of parents must register (ie nannies and other carers in your own home).

A childminder must be registered if she cares for children under age 8 in her own home for more than two hours per day for reward or payment.

Who doesn't have to register: relatives, a person employed in the parent's own home (nanny, mother's help, au pair), shared-care nanny (as long as it's just one or two sets of parents).

Many of the Act's requirements (registration, keeping records, etc) have been done all along, the difference is that now all local authorities must carry them out regularly and within a reasonable timescale.

Under The Act the local authority has a duty to inspect all registered childcare provision once a year. This is to check on the number of children and carers, the maintenance and safety of the premises and equipment, the maintenance of records on staff and children. The under-8s teams are usually supportive and encouraging.

Local authorities may add their own requirements to the nationally mandatory ones. They also create their own registration system, reviews and reports. So the basics will be the same everywhere, but there will be variations in different areas. They must publish policy statements on daycare, under-8s care, education, children in need, special educational needs and equal opportunity.

By mid-January 1993 every local authority should have completed and published a register and report on childcare provision for under-8s. The report must include a map, descriptions, policies, gaps and problem areas, and future plans. A new report must be done at least once every three years.

THE CHILDREN ACT: a chance to be heard

A main purpose of the Act is to improve the quantity and quality of childcare provision for under-8s. As well as coordinating information from official local departments (education, health, social services, leisure, etc) authorities are directed to discover local needs and problems and to ask for and to listen to input from local childcare organisations, community groups, volunteer groups, employers and parents.

Authorities also must report plans for future provision, monitoring arrangements, and cover changes in provision in the three-yearly reports. In other words they are accountable for making progress.

So now is the time, and once during every three years when the mandatory review rolls round, to speak up. Make your voice heard either as an individual or through your local WMA group, NCT, playgroup, daycare centre, childminder's group, PTA, Gingerbread group, and the like.

You can also ask your employer, if local, to state needs for provision. Contact your local county, district or borough Social Services Department and find out who to write to and when relevant meetings are held.

FINDING YOUR CARER

**Childminders/
Day Nurseries**

For lists of registered childminders and daycare nurseries consult the Social Services Department of your local authority. The Children Act says this information should also be available at local libraries, health clinics, community centres and the like. You might also consult a neighbouring authority if you live near a borough boundary, or the local authority where you work if you could commute with your child.

For childminders, you could also contact your local childminding association, if there is one. Write to the National Childminding Association for the local branch if your Under-8s department cannot help.

For childminders, get in touch a few months in advance to see what availability is like. Six weeks should be plenty of time to find and fix final details of care. For nurseries, visit and put your name on waiting lists as early as possible - even while still pregnant.

**Agencies for
mother's helps
and nannies**

This is more expensive than advertising yourself, but all the interviewing, chasing of references, etc is done for you. It is, however, wise to double check orally the references of the person whom you are considering appointing. Do not rely solely on written references. Nanny agencies are listed in Yellow Pages and many advertise in magazines like The Lady. Most provide daily or living-in nannies or mother's helps as well as short-term or one-day cover to cope with emergencies. Some agencies charge a fixed fee to employers while others ask for a percentage of the nanny's salary.

Au pairs

There are many agencies supplying au pairs, some specialising in girls from one particular country. Alternatively, find an au pair by personal recommendation, by trying contacts abroad for suggestions, or try advertising in foreign magazines. An au pair here now may know someone suitable at home, or her mother may; ask parents who are employing au pairs. Foreign churches and YM/YWCAs sometimes have au pair agencies; try the 'phone book under the nationality or ring an embassy to enquire.

**After school
schemes**

Check with your local Social Services office for a list of local after school/holiday schemes, or ask at the school where your child is, or will be attending. Schemes tend to be rare and very popular with long waiting lists so put down your child's name as soon as you know what school your child will be attending.

Play schemes and Play centres	Contact Social Services, leisure and amenities, or the education department at the Town Hall for details.
Childcare in general	There may be a local directory available from your council or one produced by a local WMA group, NCT or other voluntary organisation in your area which will list local services. In some areas there are drop-in childcare information services, such as the Brighton 'Childcare Link'.

Advertising

When	For nannies and mother's helps, you should leave yourself about six weeks to advertise for and choose your carer. Bear in mind that it may take two weeks for your advertisement to appear in a magazine, one week in a newspaper. Applicants who already have a job will have to give their employers up to a month's notice; though there will always be some (including students about to qualify) not currently employed.
Where	(a) Newsagents' windows and local noticeboards (eg local schools, playgroups, community centres, churches, One O'Clock Clubs and Childminders' centres). These can be good for finding part-time care and childminders. Remember to ensure your childminder becomes registered if you find her this way. (See page 15). Some health authorities do not allow any advertising on clinic noticeboards.

(b) Your local Job Centre. This is a useful place to advertise for daily childcare help. Details of your job will be passed on to suitably qualified job-seekers, and the service is free.

(c) The local press. This is a useful place to advertise for most types of care, except perhaps live-in nannies.

(d) Magazines and newspapers. Addresses given at the back of the book; ring them for current advertising rates.

The Lady. Comes out weekly on Wednesdays. Advertisements are not taken by telephone, and are subject to availability of space. Probably the most popular place to advertise for a live-in nanny or mother's help.

Nursery World. Comes out fortnightly. Available to qualified nannies, nurseries and nanny-training colleges.

The Independent. Classified ads Sunday and Tuesday.

(e) At colleges where nannies are trained: if you are prepared to take on someone in her first job after training you could approach a college where NNEB courses are run. Training usually ends in June. Telephone your local Further Education College and ask if they run an NNEB course.

What should the advertisement say?

The most important points to include in the advertisement are: type of work (does it include housework or just childcare?), number and ages of children, daily or living-in, any training and/or experience required. You will get some idea of suitable wording by looking at similar advertisements. Some for example, specify 'non-smoker' or 'dog-lover' or 'driving licence required'. Avoid being too specific about the person you think you want - you may deter some good applicants. Here is a sample advertisement which was successfully placed in *The Lady*:

> MOTHER'S HELP/NANNY required September for 6 month old boy Clapham area. Own room, shower. Some housework. 6 weeks paid holiday. Both parents teaching. References. Tel.-

Nannies often prefer to work in a household where both parents are out during the day, so it can be useful to indicate that this is the case. Applicants say they prefer hard facts to gushing remarks about 'lovely room' or 'adorable boy'. If you include your telephone number, you will get a great many calls. This can be quite tiring as many of the calls may be totally unsuitable. Box numbers, on the other hand, get far fewer replies, but the advantages are that it is much easier to select the candidates you want to interview, and you may attract the more serious and dedicated applicants. If you are using your home phone number be careful about giving your name and address and children's names to strangers.

Don't worry if your requirements are unusual - eg you work shift hours, mornings only, or on a freelance basis. Just specify exactly what you want. You have a good chance of finding someone who can work flexible hours to suit you.

Interviewing

Your first contact with prospective people or places who might care for your child will probably be by telephone. An organised conversation can be a useful preliminary screening that eliminates totally unsuitable carers. In order to be prepared with all your basic queries it can be useful to prepare a simple duplicated form to keep near the 'phone.

If you advertise, interview people who answer your ads as soon as possible - good candidates find other jobs rapidly. Prepare a list of candidates to interview and keep a back-up list in case you find you have to see more people. Likewise see likely childminders or nurseries as soon as you can. Places fill up and waiting lists only grow longer.

Preliminary Information

Over the 'phone (jot down the answers)

(a) Ask: name, address, experience

If it's a nanny/mother's help/au pair: qualifications, details of last job and reasons for leaving.

If it's a childminder/nursery: number of children being cared for, availability for your child.

(b) Check: that someone answering your advertisement understands the ad, or that information you have read or heard about the childminder/nursery from the Social Services register or elsewhere is correct.

(c) Tell nanny/mother's help/au pair: hours and place of work, other details of conditions (eg accommodation), number of children and their ages, pay, tax and National Insurance arrangements, duties expected.

Ask childminder/nursery: hours of opening, fees, any conditions of acceptance (must live in borough, waiting list fee etc).

(d) If you decide to proceed, arrange the interview. Or arrange to call back when you have a shortlist. Allow 45 - 60 minutes for each interview.

When you visit a childminder/nursery, go without the distraction of your child, if possible, so you can talk in depth. If all goes well, arrange a time when you can stop in with your child to see how minder, child and other children get along. Both parents should come, if possible, or else arrange a return visit for the other parent once you are close to a decision.

To interview a nanny/mother's help/au pair, tell her your address and how to reach it easily. Bear in mind that you should offer to pay her travel. Arrange the time for her to arrive and make a point of asking her to let you know if she decides not to come for the interview.

For a carer who will work in your home - and especially if she lives-in - interviews should be arranged at a time when both parents can be present. (Or both sets of parents in the case of a shared nanny.) Your child or children should also be there and you should be aware of how children and applicant react to each other. But also have some time without the children, so you can talk without interruptions.

The Interview

Experience shows that the most important consideration is the feeling that you can get on well with the person you choose, feel comfortable with her and trust her. And the same goes for an organisation. Even if you disagree on some matters you should respect each other's views. If you have very strong opinions yourself it may be better to choose a less experienced or new nanny, mother's help or childminder (or an au pair for older children), and make it clear that you will guide her. Good communication between you and your carer is essential and will directly affect your child's well-being.

Here is a list of questions you may want to discuss at the interview. Begin by checking all the basic data you gathered in your 'phone conversation. Then talk about the carer's background and ideas on childcare, and finish with formalities. A good approach is to talk through a typical day. You also might ask her for an example of a problem with a previous child (or employer) and how she resolved it. In your chat include information about both parents' work and hours and some of your own ideas or concerns about childcare. Remember that the carer is also interviewing you!

Topics to cover about children

- What are her/their ideas on play, food, social activities, books, discipline, potty training, etc for children?

- How will your child's day be filled? eg what happens on a wet afternoon?

- How well prepared is she/are they on matters of safety/first aid?

- What does she like best about caring for children?

Background - of childminder

- Her personal circumstances (ie married, children, possibly husband's job, likely not to move house)

- Her health - for instance, does she smoke?

- What sort of pets does she keep? (this or other specific items that matter to you personally)

- Is she registered; any previous experience or qualifications? (playleader training, member of National Childminders Association)

Background - of nursery/out of school scheme	- How long have they been open? - Are they registered? - Who runs the organisation, will you meet them? - How much involvement do parents have? - What times must you bring and collect your child?
Formalities - with a childminder, nursery, out-of-school scheme	- What nappies, clothes, money for outings, etc must you supply? - What about sickness, holidays? - Will you have a trial period, a settling-in time? - How much notice must you give/will you get? - What are the fees and when do you pay them? - Can you have the name, address and telephone number of other parents of children she/they care for? If not yet registered, can you have two references, including a health visitor or GP?
Background - of nanny/mother's help	- Her personal circumstances (ie single, married, children?) - Her health - does she smoke? - Her politics and religion (if these are important to you) - Previous work experience, maybe since leaving school. - Does she mind cats, dogs, etc? - What are her long term plans, if any? - How does she feel about such tasks as cooking, washing, shopping, etc? (Make it absolutely clear what you expect to be done.)
Formalities - with nanny/ mother's help	- If living-in, show her the accommodation you are providing and explain what facilities are available, eg use of 'phone, car, bathroom, kitchen. - Where will she be able to entertain her friends? - Will she eat her meals with you? - What sickness and holiday arrangements do you propose? - Will you have a trial period? - How much notice will you give and expect? - What pay are you offering/is she wanting? Explain National Insurance and tax arrangements. - What are the names, addresses and 'phone numbers of two referees? One should, where possible, be the name of her last employer.
At the end of the interview	Check that the carer has had the opportunity to ask you any questions that s/he has. Explain to a childminder or nursery that you will

be in touch very soon about taking the available place or putting your child's name on the waiting list. You may want to make an appointment for the child and other parent to visit. With a nanny or other candidate for employment explain when you will contact her with news of the outcome of her application. You might also add that if she is hired you will both sign a contract spelling out all the terms and conditions discussed at the interview. (A ready-made contract, with spaces to fill in as appropriate, is available from the Working Mothers Association.)

References

For unregistered carers (nannies, mother's helps, au pairs, not-yet-registered childminders) you MUST check at least two references, however confident you feel. Ask referees:

- When was she employed and what were her duties?
- What was she paid?
- What was her reason for leaving?
- What was her record like for sickness and general reliability?
- What were her weak points?
- (Most important) Do they recommend her?

Beware of previous employers you can't speak to, especially the last one. It may also help to speak to other parents she has worked for on a more casual basis, ie for babysitting or part-time daycare.

With registered childminders and organisations you have the assurance of the local authority's certificate and inspections, but you may still wish to talk to the local under-8s officer or other parents who use the carer just to get another point of view.

The Children Act and good childcare practice

Though things like ratio of carer-to-child and toilets-and-basins-per-child and other details are specified in The Children Act 1989, day-to-day care is not spelled out in every detail. However, guidelines of 'good practice policies' are given by which the authority should assess organisations and childminders as to quality of care.

Here are some of the guidelines. They are caring and sensible, and you might find them useful for assessing an organisation or childminder yourself. Even though the Act does not generally encompass nannies and au pairs caring for children in your own home, you might still find the recommendations a helpful guideline to discuss with them. You might even find them a good practice guide for parenting!

- The day's programme should be planned before the children arrive.

- Activities should be appropriate to the child's age and development.

- There should be a variety of activities encouraging physical, cognitive and social skills.

- Young children should have stimulating learning opportunities, including a variety of toys. For school-age children there should be visits and outings, and equipment should allow for art, collage, sport and games, dressing up, music, jigsaws, constructions toys and crafts.

- Children should be involved in planning activities.

- There should be time and space for both quiet and noisy activities.

- Children should be allowed to work at their own pace.

- There should be an agreed policy on behaviour and punishments, appropriate to the age and stage of the child's development. Corporal punishment by registered carers is illegal.

- There should be affection and sensitive responsiveness between adult and child; a child's dignity and individuality should be respected and catered for.

- Parents' input should be respected and parents should be fully informed about their child's activities.

- There should be a First Aid box and training and agreed arrangements for emergencies.

FINDING AND CHOOSING YOUR CHILDCARE - CHECKLIST

Telephone and visit nurseries or out of school schemes as soon as you decide you will go back to work. Put name on waiting lists.

Telephone suitable-sounding childminders or run nanny advertisement about six weeks before you plan to start work.

Make sure you are well clued up on going rates of pay locally.

Check the status of your carer - does she need to be registered?

Will she be an employee - in which case you must pay her tax and National Insurance - or is she eligible for self-employment?

Make sure you keep a clear record of interviews to help you remember details later.

Arrange interviews.

Check at least two references.

Evaluate interviews:
- Past experience, references.
- Ideas on childcare.
- Understanding on hours, fees, other formalities.
- Feel you can communicate with and trust carer.

Agree start date and sign Terms and Conditions or Contract.

ONCE YOU HAVE MADE YOUR CHOICE

Discuss with the person or place you have chosen final details of pay/fees and fix a starting date. As appropriate, phone or write to the other candidates you interviewed or visited.

With a nursery or childminder you may be asked to sign a contract or agreement of terms and conditions. Whether you are or not, be sure you understand policies or agree on hours to drop off/collect, holiday, sickness, payment of fees, notice required, etc.

If you are employing someone directly - ie a nanny, shared nanny or mother's help - it is advisable to prepare a written set of Conditions of Service. This should be agreed at the outset of the employment and each party should keep a copy for future reference. Although it is not in itself a legal contract, it can serve both as a useful arbiter in cases of misunderstanding and, as a last resort, would be useful evidence if litigation arose out of a dispute. Here is a guide for a set of Conditions of Service. (A ready made contract of employment - with blank spaces to fill in as appropriate - is available from the Working Mothers Association and is free to members, otherwise contact the office for the current price.)

Conditions of service

Period of employment From what starting date to when? (The latter may, of course, be open-ended.) How much notice will be given and expected?

Title and duties What is the job called? What are the duties expected? (Define as exactly as you can what household tasks you wish to be carried out, if any, as vagueness on this point can easily lead to dissatisfaction all round.)

What responsibilities are expected? (You could define here exactly what should be done in cases of emergency.)

Place Where will she work? (This will probably only arise as a question if you share a nanny or if you propose to move the whole household - for the summer, for example.)

Hours Include both total number of hours per week, and approximate starting and finishing times each day. Make it clear if any evening or weekend babysitting is included in her basic hours, and what arrangements will be made for overtime.

Pay Weekly or monthly? Explain how she will be paid and when.

Make it clear whether pay is inclusive of National Insurance contributions and income tax. When will pay be reviewed?

Accommodation and other benefits Describe what is being offered as accommodation and access to such things as television, personal shower, cooking facilities. Explain meal arrangements and use of car, if appropriate.

Holidays Explain number of days/weeks per year. Stipulate when you would prefer these to be taken and how much notice you like of holiday dates. Mention whether you expect to take her on holiday with you.

Sickness Describe what arrangements you have made about sick pay and sick leave. See Sick Pay on page 55.

Special Leave Explain under what circumstances you will give her special leave of absence.

A guide to your child

Another document - a less formal one - which is useful is a 'guide to your child' for your carer to refer to in the early stages of her employment. This is particularly useful if your child is still a very young baby. A good childminder and nursery should ask you all these things and keep records, but you may still want to write them out as a reminder to yourself. List details of:

Diet Number, timing and composition of feeds; feeding equipment used and it's care.

Personal care Creams, nappies, vitamin drops etc.

Sleeping patterns In cot, in pram, face down, with teddy etc. How long and how often?

Idiosyncrasies Special likes or fears, favourite toys etc.

Emergency contacts Work phone numbers of both parents, if possible. Phone number of doctor. Phone number of nearest casualty department plus details of how to get there.

Note on insurance

Before anyone starts work in your home on either a daily or live-in basis, you should check with your insurers that your household policy provides sufficient cover. Also check car insurance if she is to drive your car.

Ask if your childminder, nursery, etc has public liability insurance. The Children Act does not require it, but does strongly recommend it. The National Childminding Association provides its own insurance scheme for members.

Running-in period

Plan to hand over care gradually. For example, you may start by taking your child to a childminder or day nursery for half days only for a week. This can help reassure you that your child will settle down without you happily.

If you are employing a nanny, you could spend a day or two with her and then another day or so around the house, perhaps working upstairs, but basically no longer in charge.

This overlap period can be very valuable in building up your confidence in your childcare arrangements and preparing you for the inevitably emotional moment when you relinquish your totally maternal role. Probably no-one finds this moment easy but it is likely to hurt you more than the child.

If you go back to work when your child is still very young, maybe after the 28 weeks of statutory maternity leave, he or she will probably adjust to a new routine quite easily. Older children are often more clingy or may set up shrieks as you leave but they will probably be perfectly happy once they've recovered from your departure. If you phone during the day to check progress, you will almost certainly find that your child is showing no signs of pining for you!

MAKING IT WORK

Childminder

If you have a childminder, suggest tactfully that she joins a local Childminders Group if she doesn't already belong to one. This will keep her in touch with news on toy libraries, local playgroups, One O'Clock Clubs etc. (One O'Clock Clubs are free informal afternoon playgroups for under-fives run by local authority recreation departments usually in parks or playgrounds.)

Nanny

If you have a nanny and she is new to your area help her to make contact with other nannies locally. You can do this by 'phoning other mothers and initiating small get-togethers. You could also try advertising in newsletters produced by local WMA or National Childbirth Trust groups, or introduce her to courses at the local adult education institute. Encourage your nanny to take your child to meet other children and to go on outings. Introduce her to local One O'Clock Clubs or mother and toddler groups. Arrange for her to take your child to the clinic for regular routine check-ups.

At the end of the day

Although the morning handover will almost inevitably be a rushed one, the afternoon one should be a time for a mutual exchange of views and information on your child's welfare. Reports on food, sleeping, health etc, will become routine, but a more thorough exploration of ideas on your child's development will be valuable from time to time. Some mothers, especially of young babies, find a simple chart, filled in by the nanny or childminder, a useful device for keeping them thoroughly informed. This can help them plan weekend timetables and diet to suit the child's weekday pattern. It is important to explain that the intention is not to be either bureaucratic or prying!

A last word

Whoever cares for your child, it is worth reminding yourself not to take the person or the organisation for granted. Be constantly considerate about consulting first if you have to change your usual arrangements; strenuously avoid exploiting good nature; give as much notice as possible of your holidays; review pay from time to time; don't forget to say how much efforts are appreciated. All this may sound insultingly obvious, but these points are vital to the good working relationship which will benefit all of you, including your child.

Contingency cover

However carefully you've arranged your childcare, it may, at times, fall apart. The nanny or mother's help gets ill or suddenly quits, the childminder has her own family crisis or her holiday, the nursery or school closes because the heating has failed or there's a staff training day... You need to have backup and it's a good idea to think about it now. The easiest solution may be to call on a support network you have developed for yourself, including:

Other mothers

On maternity leave or when you are not working, in antenatal clinics and exercise classes, in hospital, at baby clinics and mother-and-baby groups, at playgroups, nursery, school...get to know other mothers. You have your children in common, so striking up conversations is easy. Arrange to meet each other, arrange for the children to play together, cultivate friendships by inviting children on outings, having older children to sleep over night, babysitting for each other, etc. These mums, be they working or full-time at home, are your network of community information (about schools, dentists, children's clothes shops, etc). They are also your fall-back system when you need one, able to collect your child from school, or take your child for a day or half-day or possibly longer. It's best if you can return the favour in some way, or pay it back by taking their child for a Saturday or some such.

Neighbours

People who live nearby, even if they don't have young children, can often be the handiest to ask for simple help. The acquaintance develops naturally when you chat over the fence, walk down the street together, queue at the local shops. Or you might join or start a neighbourhood watch scheme.

Working parents groups	Join or start one in your area (membership of the WMA puts you in touch with a local group automatically, address at back of book). You not only have parenting in common, but the challenges of combining work and parenting. Most groups meet once a month. Some have speakers or local experts on various parenting subjects. The main point is to get to know each other so you can pool your resources when a domestic crisis strikes.
Nanny/au pair network	If you have a nanny, mother's help or au pair, get to know other families nearby who do, too, even if you have to advertise in a local newsletter or shop window. You'll be helping her to make friends, and if the friendships flourish reasonably well (including between you, the other family and all children) these carers may be able to help out in an emergency. Even if you don't have a nanny/au pair yourself, you may be able to ask one nearby to help out. You should, of course, offer to pay in these circumstances.
Childminder support	Check that your childminder has ties with the local childminding organisation or other minders (a good reason she should join the NCMA). They often make agreements to help each other out in case of illness or emergency. Some local authority Social Services back up childminders in this way.

If your carefully cultivated network of support falls through or is not suitable, say if your child is ill, there are other possibilities:

You may be entitled to Family Leave or compassionate leave; check to see if your employer offers these. If not, you may be able to take holiday leave or unpaid leave.

Your partner may be allowed Family Leave or compassionate leave, or may be able to take holiday or unpaid leave or may more easily be able to take some time off.

A relative (grandparent, sister...) might be able to fill in, even if they normally have commitments that keep them from being your regular carer.

One expensive solution is to use a commercial childcare agency (found in larger towns and cities; look under Nurses or Employment Agencies in the Yellow Pages).

In some circumstances, a temporary childminder may be able to step in.

Could you possibly bring your (well) child in to work with you? It depends on the work you do and the age and behaviour of your child. On the other hand, can you do work at home, just for a day (few days)?

EMERGENCY CARE CHECKLIST

Family or Compassionate Leave for you (or your partner).

Grandparent or other relative.

Local non-employed friend with child your own child's age.

Local working parent with nanny/au pair.

Neighbour.

Friend of your childminder/au pair/nanny.

Holiday Leave.

Agency nanny or nurse.

Temporary Registered childminder.

THE FORMALITIES

Rates mentioned are given as examples only, as they usually change every year, sometimes more often. For current figures, ring your local tax, PAYE office, or Social Security Contributions Agency. Members of WMA receive regular updates on the costs and formalities of carers via the Newsletter.

Giving notice Unless circumstances are exceptional, give as much notice as you can. A childminder will accept a minimum of one week's notice, but would obviously prefer enough time to organise a replacement for your child.

Most nurseries will stipulate required notice - one week to one month. Out of school schemes vary depending on how formally they are run.

Nannies and mother's helps: you should explain this in her conditions of service (see page 45). By law you would be expected to give or receive a week's notice in the first year of her employment, two weeks for the next year and longer thereafter. You can also fix the length of the contract, for example one year, and renew it if you both want to continue.

The self-employed nanny If you are employing someone in your home and paying her more than the current 'lower earnings limit' (if it's a live-in or daily nanny you probably are) then by law you must deduct her tax and NI and pay them in through a PAYE scheme. Some nannies claim to be self-employed, wanting to be paid in cash, and some parents gratefully accept this, but it is very doubtful that they would pass the Inland Revenue's tests, and you as the employer are liable for her payment. You could be fined and made to pay any employer's NI contribution owing.

If your prospective nanny wants to try for self-employed status you could ring your local tax office to enquire about applying for it, as rulings can vary, but it would only be likely if, say, she worked for three families flexibly. In one of their booklets it states that the "Inspector of Taxes...will want to establish that you (ie the nanny) are in control of the way in which the business is run". If your employee can tell when she wants to work rather than you specifying her hours then perhaps she is self-employed, but this seems unlikely. It may be worth pointing out that self-employed people miss out on many benefits such as unemployment pay and will not get paid holidays, and that an employee is covered by National Insurance for accidents at work ('Industrial injuries'). If your employee earns too little to pay tax she can still keep up her entitlement to some benefits by paying voluntary contributions (class 3); get leaflet NI42 from the DSS offices.

Childminders have self-employed status, so it is up to your childminder to manage her tax affairs. If you have found someone who is new to childminding, encourage her to set herself up properly. The National Childminding Association will help her, and so may the local Under-8s team.

Tax and National Insurance

If you are going to pay tax for your employee, there are a number of things you have to do. It sounds complicated, but the officers at the PAYE tax office and Department of Social Security (Contributions Agency) can be very helpful over the telephone. In brief, you have to deduct her NI contribution and her income tax from her pay, and you yourself have to pay the employer's NI contribution. Then once a quarter you will need to spend some time working out the total of your NI contributions plus her tax and NI contributions, which you pay direct to the Inland Revenue, either by post or through the bank. If you complete the Deductions Card each time you pay her you can easily add up the quarterly totals. (By law you must give your employee a payslip each time she is paid, setting out the deductions from gross pay.) Finally at the end of the tax year, in early April, you will be sent a new Deduction Card and asked to return the old one. You are not required to complete a P60.

When you want to employ someone, contact your Inland Revenue PAYE tax office (address in the 'phone directory or 'phone your local tax enquiry office and ask them for the telephone number). Ask for the 'Employers Control Section' and explain that you are employing just one person and want to pay tax under the Simplified Deduction Scheme. They also call it a domestic scheme or a QD scheme. They will probably ask what you intend to pay, to find out if it is above the lower earnings limit. They'll be able to tell you the deduction amounts over the 'phone, and they'll arrange to send you a starter pack and issue you with a tax office reference number.

Some local tax offices are more familiar with the Simplified Deduction Scheme than others. If you are asked to operate the regular PAYE scheme and complete a P60, or if you receive irrelevant documents such as the 'Employers Guide to PAYE', or P11 deduction cards, get back in touch with your tax office to ensure you get into the correct PAYE system.

The following example is a guide to help you calculate the actual cost to you of employing someone. Many prospective employees expect to know what they will receive as net pay so you may find the example useful to show them how much they will get in their pay packets. We started by saying we would pay about £100 'in hand' and filled in the other amounts required via a quick telephone call to our local PAYE office. These amounts will change every year, and so may the salary, so use this same guide to work it out for yourself.

Ideally, it is best to agree on a gross pay figure (based on what you know you can afford) rather than agree a net, 'cash in hand' amount which you will then have to honour, regardless of variables in 'free pay' and NI contributions (which may push up the gross pay to more than you had budgeted for).

EXAMPLE

TO FIGURE WEEKLY NET PAY, GROSS PAY AND TOTAL COST TO YOU

(1993/94 tax year - April 1st to March 31st - deductions supplied from PAYE office and tax and NI tables)

£100.00   Nanny's pay in hand per week after deductions.

£10.09   Nanny's tax, based on the current tax code, assuming she is single with no dependents. The tax code, which changes every year, says how much of her income is 'free pay' (not taxed); she must pay tax on her gross pay above that amount.

Code for tax year 1993/94 is 344L, with 'free pay' of £66.33. Gross pay above this is taxed at 20% up to £48pw and 25% over £48pw.

£6.56   Nanny's National Insurance contribution, based on pay level. This, like income tax, has a lower earnings limit below which NI does not have to be paid (may be different to the tax limit).

£116.65   Nanny's gross pay before deductions.

£7.69   Employer's National Insurance contribution. This, like the employee's contribution changes every year.

£124.34   Cost to you, the employer, weekly. BUT you only pay out the pay in hand after deductions (the figure at the top of our example), filling in the amounts of deductions weekly on the Deductions Card (P12) supplied to you by the PAYE office. You total these amounts every quarter and pay the total in.

EXAMPLE: TO FIGURE QUARTERLY PAYE TAX AND NI CONTRIBUTIONS PAYMENTS

£10.09		Nanny's weekly tax
	£131.17	x 13 weeks
£6.56		Nanny's weekly NI contribution
	£85.28	x 13 weeks
£7.69		Employer's weekly NI contribution
	£99.97	x 13 weeks
	£316.42	Employer's quarterly payment to PAYE. Note, this is not extra to the calculations above. It's just what tax and NI come to on a quarterly basis; in other words, the amount of the cheque you'll have to pay in. This should all be clear when you receive your Deduction Card (P12) and Simplified Deduction Scheme instructions (P16).

When she starts Ask your nanny if she has a P45 ('Employee Leaving - copy of employer certificate') from her previous job. If she was a domestic nanny in her last job, she won't have this, but she should give you her previous employer's Simplified PAYE reference number. If she doesn't have that, you just need her name, address and NI number. Supply these to the PAYE office you spoke to. You should get back from them, possibly in a useful folder called New Employers Starter Pack - Simplified Scheme (P4Q) the following documents which are often referred to by their code numbers:

(a) Form P16A. This should be returned straight away giving details of the employee. A P12 deduction card will then be issued.

(b) Simplified tax tables (P16); this is a folded card with instructions on how to fill in the deduction card, and a table for you to work out the right tax once you know the employee's 'free pay'.

(c) National Insurance Contribution tables (CF7). This booklet is reprinted each time there is a change in NI rates. The period of validity is stated in the CF7 NI table.

(d) A book of payslips to send with your quarterly cheque (sent to the Collector of Taxes, not the Inspector: you will be given envelopes too).

NB - Even if you have not received the documents yet, you must begin making deductions from the start of employment. If necessary, agree provisional figures over the phone with your tax office.

You will also be sent booklets about Statutory Sick Pay (SSP), Statutory Maternity Pay (SMP) and an Employer's Guide to NI. Keep these until you need to refer to them. In addition, you will be advised of any change in 'free pay' (which usually changes after the budget) or tax tables, some weeks after they have been announced (if not, phone your tax office).

When she leaves Add up the totals on the Deduction Card (P12) to the date of leaving and pay in to the Accounts Office any tax and NI contributions due. Fill in the information requested on the back of the deduction card and send to the Inspector. Give the nanny your PAYE reference number. No P45 is required under the Simplified Deduction Scheme.

Sick Pay The state scheme provides Statutory Sick Pay for employees who qualify. You, the employer, must pay a set amount of sick pay and then claim back 80% of this from your regular NI/PAYE payments. This only applies to you if you are paying in tax and NI as outlined above. It does not apply if the employee is paid less than the lower earnings limit (the amount usually changes each year). Contracts of less than three months are also exempted. Many working mothers who employ nannies will already have formal arrangements about sick pay as part of their original employment agreement (eg you may offer two weeks full pay in addition to any state benefits).

Here are a few points about SSP. Should you need to pay it see the booklets supplied with your PAYE scheme, plus the employers Quick Guide (NI268, updated yearly) and ring your local Department of Social Security.

Who is eligible? All employees whether full or part-time (even after one day's employment) who earn over the lower earnings limit. Exceptions: those of pensionable age, on maternity benefit, in receipt of certain state benefits in the last 57 days.

When eligible? If ill for four days in a row (or more, up to 28 weeks in a year), but SSP is not payable until after the first three days, called 'waiting days'. Only working days are counted. There are special ways to calculate the PIW (period of incapacity for work), and whether or not it links with previous PIWs.

How do I know she is ill? A doctor's certificate is only available for absences of 7 days or more. You can ask for a 'self certificate' (a note from the employee). Keep a notebook with details of absences, phone calls and reasons in case she does not provide GP's or self certificates.

How much do I pay? You only pay for 'qualifying days'. There are two SSP rates, depending on your nanny's average weekly earnings. The lower and upper earnings limits and the SSP rates payable usually change each year. Tax and NI contributions still must be deducted, if applicable.

How do I get my money back? You get back 80% of the total gross SSP you have paid. You deduct it from your quarterly totals and payment on your PAYE Deduction Card (P12).

The DSS will require you to keep records of days usually worked, days of sickness, and payments made and not made, with reasons. If you do not request self-certification it may be worthwhile keeping a notebook with details of absences, phone calls and reasons.

Maternity pay

You must also pay your nanny Statutory Maternity Pay if she earns more than the lower earnings limit and has worked for you for 26 weeks or more by 15 weeks before the baby is due. SMP is 100% reclaimable from your NI/PAYE payments. To work out dates and amounts see the booklets mentioned above which came with your PAYE pack, and contact your Department of Social Security office.

Help

Keep records of everything to do with your nanny's work, time off, pay and deductions week by week, etc. Do this in addition to the payslip and Deduction Card.

If you make a mistake in contributions you can put it right in the next quarterly payment, or at the end of the tax year. If you have already sent in the Deduction Card ask the PAYE inspector if you can still make an adjustment. If it is too late, ask your local Social Security office.

Keep your records for three years or longer. You may be asked for information or evidence about nannies long after they have left.

If you are perplexed, talk it over with your PAYE office or local Department of Social Security, also known (on the paying in end) as the Contributions Agency or phone (free) for advice on Social Security (ie NI and Sick Pay) 0800 393 539.

You may also be able to get advice from another more experienced parent who employs a nanny or through someone at your local WMA group.

FORMALITIES CHECKLIST

FOR A CHILDMINDER OR NURSERY:

Make sure you are aware of any conditions they may have, eg period of notice, increase in fees.

Do they have adequate insurance cover and is their registration current with the Social Services Department?

For a childminder it is a good idea for you to have a written agreement regarding holiday/sick pay, overtime etc.

FOR A NANNY:

Telephone the PAYE tax office to find out what tax and National Insurance you must deduct from weekly pay. Ask for Simplified Deduction Scheme forms and booklets.

Sign Contract or agree Conditions of Service with nanny.

Check your insurance.

Start a notebook and file for all employee work records and tax, NI and other formal paperwork.

Telephone your PAYE office if you find the paperwork confusing.

Write out a guide to your child and discuss with nanny.

Allow time for running-in period.

Start your work and give a deserving new carer flowers and praise at the end of your first week.

AT WORK

Over recent years a number of employers have initiated new, flexible work patterns. Some have pioneered various forms of subsidised childcare. If you are not fortunate enough to work for one of these companies - and they are still the exception - you may find your employer is open to individual arrangements along these lines, if you ask for them. Some of these variations can actually save money for an employer, as well as make combining family and work easier for you. It makes economic sense for employers to retain experienced trained employees regardless of the economic climate.

Before and During Your Baby Break

Maternity Leave and Rights

Every pregnant woman is legally entitled to paid time off for antenatal appointments. Currently (watch for changes after October 1994), if she qualifies, a pregnant woman who works up to 11 weeks before the birth of her child has the right to return to existing employment up to 29 weeks following the birth. This amounts to a possible total of 40 weeks maternity leave. 'Existing employment' means reinstatement on similar terms and conditions and does not necessarily mean the same job. To qualify, you must have worked for the same employer for 16 hours or more per week for two years, or 8 - 16 hours per week for five years. Employers of less than five people are exempt when not reasonably practicable.

With similar sorts of qualifications about length of service, employers must pay Statutory Maternity Pay for 18 weeks of maternity leave whether or not you intend to return to work. This is 90% of your earnings for the first six weeks, then it drops to a lower flat rate for the remaining 12 weeks. If you don't fully qualify, you receive the flat rate for 18 weeks. Self-employed women, if they qualify by having made National Insurance contributions, can receive State Maternity Allowance which is a bit less than the lower SMP rate.

There are certain time limits for taking maternity leave and for notifying your employer of your intention to take it and to return to work; sometimes this has to be in writing. Check details with your personnel officer, the local Social Services Department or your antenatal clinic.

Some employers offer more generous terms than the legal requirements, such as shortening the time for eligibility, allowing a longer break or giving better maternity pay. Individual employers may have restrictions on certain employee benefits, ie service time, payments towards pensions, private health insurance cover or cheap mortgages or loans. Some disallow these, or link them to conditions about returning to work.

(Note! If you are employing a nanny or mother's help for two years or more, and she becomes pregnant, then she should have paid maternity leave. You reclaim the money from the Department of Social Security. Contact your local Social Security office for help and information.)

Career Break Some employers guarantee re-employment at the same level at which you leave, with a re-training programme on return. Usually a minimum number of years of full-time service is required, and some employers limit the offer to employees with certain skills or management potential. Others, especially local authorities, may offer career breaks to all staff. There is usually a limit to the number of years off you can take. The employer might require you to work for a minimum of two weeks a year, say, and attend an annual one-day seminar. You might be sent information packs, journals and reports, invited to local social events, and be encouraged to study in your field. Sometimes professional subscriptions and conference expenses are paid by the employer.

'Reservist' schemes give no guarantees of a job, but do consider you for re-employment. The break for these can be longer and there is less contact during the break.

Maternity Packs Some employers provide information on maternity leave. A supportive company may provide wider information, including guidance and help in finding local childcare. Some also offer a workshop, like the WMA's 'Taking Maternity Leave', which covers work and pregnancy, maternity benefits, changing relationships, childcare considerations and other topics.

Paternity Leave Some employers now offer men official paid paternity leave: time off at or near the time of their child's birth of 2 - 10 days, sometimes longer. There may be some service requirement. Other fathers have to use their holiday entitlement or take unpaid leave.

Keeping in Touch Work can seem remote when you are on maternity leave. The radical change brought by coping with a baby, and being at home all day can contribute to a loss of confidence and perspective, which is why many women decide not to go back to work. Some employers support their employees on maternity leave in the following ways (if yours does not, you might consider arranging these yourself):

- Company literature - staff newsletters, major reports - sent to you at home.

- Professional membership fees and subscriptions to journals kept up. If the company doesn't do this, they would probably send back issues on to you.

- Briefing and settling-in time when you return, especially if it is a new job or anything has changed at the old one.

- A course or workshop - the WMA runs one called 'Back to Work', which covers the practicalities and feelings involved in combining work and childcare. At the very least talk to a colleague who is on or has returned from maternity leave, or contact other working mothers through the WMA.

Retraining and Refresher Courses Whether you are returning to the same job at the same organisation or picking up a career again after years away, it's a good idea, and sometimes essential, to brush up on skills and knowledge. Your old or new employer or professional association might provide a course. Some employment agencies offer courses to update office skills. Women's magazines, radio stations, women-and-work exhibitions are other sources of information on retraining. The Women Returners Network (address at back of book) provides comprehensive information on courses around the country.

BACK AT WORK

Breastfeeding at Work If your company offers a workplace nursery you can breastfeed during the lunch break. But this situation is rare. Most women who wish to continue breastfeeding express milk at work during the day for the baby to drink the next day. Ideal employers provide a quiet, private, non-smoking room where mothers can do this. Most women still have to do it in the toilets or in their office (if they have one!) behind closed doors. A fridge at work and a cool-bag for transport are essential.

Parental and Family Leave Most EEC countries offer these two forms of leave entitlement, but Britain has not accepted them yet. Parental Leave (not paternity leave) allows either parent to look after a child up to age two. For instance, a father could stay at home to smooth the transition when a mother starts work, or when she works her annual Career Break requirements or attends courses. A working mother could take time off legitimately if the childminder fell ill or the nanny walked out. A child's or carer's illness is usually covered by Family Leave, where offered. This is an annual quota of 3 - 10 days to cover such domestic crises. In most cases, however, parents rely on the tolerance and compassion of their employers and individual managers, or use their annual holiday leave or take unpaid leave.

In-House Support Groups Some employers encourage working parents to form self-help groups to share experiences and support each other. The WMA grew out of such groups within local communities (there are now over 150 around the UK). It is just as useful to compare notes with colleagues with whom you may have even more in common than neighbouring parents. Established workplace parents' groups usually meet once a month in the lunch hour to swap notes on all aspects of bringing up children. Some have a crisis register for when childcare fails. Suggestions for improving employment practices can arise out of these informal discussions. If you want to start such a group, send for our leaflet 'Setting Up A Local Group'.

Employer Childcare

Workplace nurseries Employers can buy places in an existing nursery, set up a nursery jointly with other employers in the area, or set up their own workplace facility, possibly run by an outside nursery company.

The cost of these nurseries is subsidised by the employer, with the parents paying less than the fees for a similar private nursery, sometimes on a sliding scale according to salary or needs. There should be a clear policy on what happens to your child's place if you leave your job.

The organisation Working for Childcare and its offshoot consultancy, Working for Childcare Ltd, helps employers set up workplace childcare (see address at back of book).

Childcare Allowances Some employers offer an allowance towards childcare costs. It may be means-tested and to be used for approved forms of under-5s care (ie registered childminder, nursery or after school scheme). It may be a straight payment or in the form of Childcare Vouchers or Childcare Cheques (see addresses at back of book). The carer exchanges the vouchers in part or full payment of the childcare fees. The Childcare Vouchers scheme provides information packs, a telephone hotline and free membership of the WMA to individual parents.

Out of School and Holiday Schemes Where these exist, the initiative has usually come from employee parents. The employers provide a grant and consult local council leisure or community services departments, the local education authority or a local sports centre to find space and help set up the scheme. Parents usually pay a fee per day, with a reduction for more than one child. Employers may join with other local employers to start a scheme, or give help to existing schemes, perhaps providing premises, or grants for equipment or staff.

The Kids' Clubs Network produces an excellent publication called Childcare for School Age Children: an Employers and Employees Guide. Kids' Clubs also run a consultancy service, the Out of School Childcare Service, to assist setting up schemes (address at back of book).

The Children Act and Workplace Childcare

Under The Children Act '89 all workplace childcare for under-8s must be registered with Social Services, and inspected once a year. This should be regarded as a source of support. One main purpose of The Act is to help employers and parents provide for childcare needs by ensuring quality of care, supporting initiatives and coordinating information.

Employer Childcare and Tax

At the time of going to press, childcare vouchers are taxable as 'perks'. The benefit is greatest if you pay very little tax. You do not have to pay National Insurance Contributions on the value of the subsidy.

Example: A £30 monthly childcare subsidy is calculated thus:

£30 x 12 months = £360 added to your income, which is then taxed at 25% if you earn in the lower tax bracket. That amounts to £90 in tax payable yearly. On a monthly basis, this means that your £30 allowance is really worth only £22.50.

Workplace nurseries, be they in-house or shared with other local employers are NOT taxed as perks. Likewise an out of school or holiday play facility provided by your employer will not be a taxable item. This tax break was introduced in the Finance Act of 1990 to encourage employers to set up new facilities. It does not apply if your employer pays a contribution to your childcare costs at a privately run nursery or afterschool scheme where it has no representation on the management.

Employer Tax Benefits

There are additional tax advantages for employers who provide childcare:

- They can offset the value of any employee childcare subsidy against tax on profits.

- Day to day running costs of a workplace nursery (wages, rent, heat and light, etc) are eligible for deduction, and so are capital costs of permanent equipment, along with other allowances.

- One of the greatest benefits to employers who provide childcare assistance is the retention of experienced employees. A cost/benefit analysis may be able to prove that potential savings in recruitment and training costs more than offset the cost of a nursery or allowance.

Other ideas

Other policies and provisions some employers offer include:

- Adoption leave on the same terms as maternity leave.

- Information and referral service on local childcare; an officer who visits childminders and nurseries and helps match parents' and children's needs to suitable carers.

- 'Temp' carers or subsidies to cover times when your childcare falls through or when your child is mildly ill.

- Babysitting allowances for late meetings or residential courses.

- Mobile creches for use during training courses or playbuses for use as holiday schemes.

Changing Work Patterns

Change in patterns of working requires new thinking on the part of employers and often on the part of employees. Some companies have existing policies, others may have to be actively encouraged to try new ways to work.

Organisations that can help you and your employers change working patterns include WMA, New Ways to Work, Equal Opportunities Commission, The Pepperell Unit (addresses at back of book).

Flexi-time

If you could start work an hour or even a half hour after the usual time it might allow you to drop your child at school instead of finding someone to do it. Or perhaps you (or your partner) could come to work an hour earlier than normal in order to leave an hour earlier to collect your child. A fair number of companies offer flexi-time, usually with 'core hours' when everyone should be at work, say 10.00am - 4.00pm. Employers generally prefer that you choose your hours, say 8.00am - 4.00pm or 10.00am - 6.00pm, and stick to them. Some let employees save up time by working extra hours.

Term-Time Working

Staff have the same conditions of service as other employees, but are allowed unpaid leave during school holidays. These periods are covered by rescheduling work or taking in temporary replacements, for instance, students on vacation.

Part-Time	Many working mothers struggle on in a full-time job, afraid to lose career prospects but having difficulty coping with home responsibilities. If your employers value you, they might be open to a rational proposal on ways you can reduce your hours but retain seniority.
Job-Sharing	This is when two people divide one full-time job between them. Pay, holidays and other benefits are also divided. Teachers, nurses, television and radio producers, librarians, medical consultants, civil servants, press officers, training managers, and telephonists are among women already doing such job-sharing. It can work in several ways.
	Two workers may do two and a half days a week each, or one may work mornings, the other afternoons, or the two may alternate weeks. Some employers stipulate that sharers have some overlap, so information is shared face to face and both are available for staff meetings. Any arrangements can work, as long as all parties agree. Job-sharing offers advantages to the employer, who benefits from two-for-the-price-of-one.
Negotiating Job-Sharing and Part-Time	You can apply to job-share a post even if the option has not been suggested. It is useful if you can provide your own partner, but not always necessary. If the job-share is your own suggestion, or if you want to do a full-time job part-time, think through the implications thoroughly and perhaps present a written proposal. Be sure to work more than 16 hours a week in order to hold on to employment protection rights and company benefits. (New Ways to Work (address at back of book) can give you lots of help on how to negotiate a job-share and/or find a partner.)
	Joining the WMA can be a good way of keeping in touch with other working mothers - perhaps even in your field - who have successfully negotiated job-share or part-time and can give you tips.
Working from Home	Not everyone has the self-discipline to work at home. There are domestic distractions, and it can be lonely. But when clear goals and standards of achievement are set it can be efficient and flexible. Traditional homeworkers do manufacturing out-work (fashion, toys, novelties). White collar homework includes jobs in publishing (illustrating, proof-reading) and clerical work (envelope addressing by hand, copy-typing, word-processing). 'Teleworkers' (using computers and phone-links supplied by employers) are the newest and still the smallest sector of professional homeworkers.
	Homeworking works best when the employer gives you support by including you in their network via newsletters and memos, and

holding regular staff meetings and training (so you will need some childcare).

An alternative is to work for yourself. If you go freelance (ie temp secretarial, accountant, physiotherapist, journalist, graphic artist) you must have more than one client to maintain your freelance status with the tax inspector. Or you could start your own business if you have the entrepreneurial spirit. (Home-Run and OwnBase are newsletters especially for those who work from home - see addresses at back of book.)

Tips on homeworking

- It's best to have a space reserved for work.

- You do need childcare for under-5s and out of school times.

- You need to know when to stop!

Persuading your employer

If your employers do not offer parent-friendly provisions perhaps you can win them over with ideas and information. What is top priority and most realistic to ask for? How do your colleagues feel? Can your union or professional body help? It could be career breaks or flexi-time, paternity leave, breastfeeding facilities or a childcare allowance, or all of these and more - whatever you, and your in-house group of employee parents, are willing to help organise and propose. In addition to winning the loyalty of working parents and saving on recruiting and re-training, employers also receive some direct tax advantages for making work-and-family life better for employees, and it is worth stating these.

Be sure your employer is aware that policies and provisions like these also create good will and a good image for the employer in the workplace, in the local community, and among competitors. This is also useful for working parents: lots of praise and publicity for creative initiatives make it difficult for employers to stop offering them!

Our publication, *The Employer's Guide to Childcare*, may be a good starting point for employers who want to know more. Further information, support and practical help is available from any of the organisations named in this section (addresses at back of book).

Employer's Initiatives Checklist

Do they offer...

Maternity packs; clear information on maternity pay and leave.

Additional supportive information.

More than basic maternity rights.

Career Break scheme.

Paternity Leave. Parental Leave. Family Leave.

Contact during maternity leave.

Refresher courses, retraining, workshops on re-entering work.

Information or referral officer on local childcare.

Breastfeeding facilities.

Workplace parent support group.

Workplace nursery, daycare centre or childcare allowance.

Workplace out of school schemes.

Holiday play schemes.

Flexi-time or job-sharing.

Term-time, part-time or home working.

Opportunities for career progression and training for part-time workers and job-sharers.

Are benefits open to all levels of the workforce?

PERSONAL EXPERIENCES

Back to Work

Kate

When I just had Rosie to look after I took her to a childminder - easily the cheapest alternative, and happily for me my childminder lived next door. No Lego under the cushion or rattles jammed behind the piano; solely time for play when we got home. It sounds wonderful, but there were still all the nappies to wash, the bath to run, the story to read and the supper to cook.

Now I have two children, quite a different ball game. Rosie (3) needs to go to a playgroup - how else do you burn off all those calories? How could a childminder cope with doing the playgroup rota, as well as looking after her own children and my two? Deciding on the line of least resistance, I opted for my own nanny. When people ask me who looks after the children, I find all sorts of excuses for having a nanny: 'It's not as posh as it sounds', I add hastily. Sometimes I don't even say I have a nanny; 'a girl' is a fairly neutral statement. Having a nanny seems to be a symbol of your financial/social status and people can make all sorts of (incorrect) assumptions about you when they know you have one.

My day: I get up at 7.00 to feed baby James and my husband gets up to wake Rosie, if she is not already awake, then get the tea and assorted drinks for the family in bed. For the next 45 minutes we all sit in bed, play and chat. at 7.45 we make a start on dressing and washing Rosie, which take about 20 minutes. (This week she has been a horse every morning and we have to catch her before we can dress her.) In theory, by 8.15 we should be on our way downstairs, having made the bed and tidied the bedroom and bathroom. I sometimes manage to eat a piece of toast and start the children's breakfast and by 8.30 Deborah starts and I leave. I get home at 5.45 by which time Rosie and James have had their tea and are ready for bath and bed.

I find this time of the day the worst as they are tired and I am irritated by them, but we usually manage to get them into bed by 7.30. However, all the children's clothes are washed, ironed and neatly put away and most of the toys are in their correct place.

Nurseries: Best form of childcare?

Dorothy

My chief memory of the two years Ben was at his nursery (and I may as well get the disadvantages over first) was the constant rush. In the morning - a rush to get up, breastfeed the baby and THEN give him a proper breakfast, take the dog for a walk, get all togged up for the journey, walk to the station, bundle baby and pushchair up the stairs and on to train, race across Waterloo Bridge pushing the buggy and eventually get him into the nursery. From there it was still a ten minute walk to work when I could eventually relax until 5.15 when the process began again in reverse.

The nursery was a private one in Covent Garden, the Chandos Day Nursery, which was entirely run by a management committee of the parents and was totally non-profitmaking. Despite that, it cost about £200 a month until your child was 2 and then slightly less. The cost combined with the events mentioned above was, for me, the chief disadvantage. You can't afford to command a salary that makes that sort of outlay worthwhile (especially doubled as it would be with the second child) if you're arriving exhausted at 9.30 and, more important, have to leave sharp at 5.15 every afternoon. I sometimes brought Ben back to work in the evening but that doesn't do much for your credibility either, especially if your boss happens to be the sort of dynamic creature who believes a woman's place is in the bed. If my husband had been doing a more ordinary 9-5 job (but he's a journalist) and could have collected occasionally, it might have been easier - other parents managed to share more efficiently. But in our case it was very difficult.

I've made it sound dreadful from start to finish but that's because I wanted to get the disadvantages out of the way so that I could wax lyrical. My overwhelming feeling is that a nursery is the best form of childcare and I feel guilty that the second one will not have that start in life. If I could afford it and there was one in easy reach, she definitely would.

From the moment Ben, at six months old, joined the nursery he was completely happy - perhaps even more so than he had been with the pair of inexperienced paranoiacs that he'd been left with before (us). He had an instant set of friends and a wide selection of toys of all different sorts. He had a team of enthusiastic, fully trained girls looking after him - all very loving and stimulating in different ways. Right from the start, he simply enjoyed being in the company of other children and getting plenty of stimulation from that. The older children benefit from learning to be gentle and caring with the younger ones who in turn discover the tricks of the trade from the older ones. Ben was always far more advanced than other, non-nursery children of his age and, although I'm not necessarily advocating pushing a child to 'learn', anyone who has watched a child grow up will know that the sooner he understands and can cope with the 'adult' world, the happier he is. Look at those awful frustrating times when he can't quite crawl, can't quite walk, can't quite talk. These all pass faster and less agonisingly if he is in the constant company of someone who is only just ahead of him, not miles up above.

The other great advantage is that they have to mix in society sooner or later, however introverted they might be, and who's to say what is the ideal age? Ben has almost always been good at sharing, good at meeting new people, good about eating and drinking in company and wonderfully gentle and understanding with his new sister. I very much doubt if he's naturally an angel - I give all the credit to the nursery. Other children go through the agony of discovering their relatively unimportant role in 'society' at 3, 4 or 5 when it really is agony. He just slipped into it quite naturally at 6 months.

Enough philosophy - the main thing was that he loved it. It was positive - somewhere to go, something new every day, a place of his own. Projects, parties, outings. Gym every Thursday, trips to the library and, most important, plenty of love. (In the two years we were there, incidentally, only one member of staff left and she had been there since the nursery started.)

Everybody else loved it too. It was happy, friendly and fun and I was completely happy about his welfare every moment he was there.

Coping With Childcare

Blossom

Having been offered a place on a full time commercial course at her local College of Further Education, Blossom, who has two school age children plus a two year old, applied for a place in the college nursery for her youngest child. She was too late to get a place there so contacted the Social Services about a Council day nursery place. Initially she was told that these too were full up but at the last minute, just as she was about to turn down her college place, the nursery rang to say that a place was available. These are her comments having just started:

"If you are lucky enough to find one, a nursery is a good place for your child. In the nursery at least you know that your child is looked after by trained staff. It is important to let your child take time and get settled before you engage yourself in your commitments. Don't be put off if he/she is upset at first. Get to know the staff and other children, if your child sees that you have got confidence in someone, they will feel the same. Try and get involved with the nursery as this will help your child to settle in even more quickly.

During the settling in period, try not to shadow your child. Let him/her discover and learn from the staff and other children what is going on. Take the settling in slowly and before you leave explain that you will be back at a certain time. If you have other children who go to school, don't panic - if you organise yourself you can do it: Try and stick to your routine, send the children to bed early, get their clothes ready for the next day, work out a time table, giving yourself a certain time to leave the house each morning.

The important thing to remember when your children are away from you all day, is to find out from them how their day went. Try to set aside a day at the week-end when you can take them somewhere interesting such as the library or park. Whatever you decide to do, once your child is happy and you are happy, I believe that you will succeed."

"The Key is Having a Routine"

Jenine

Before I returned to work I had many illusions about finding the perfect childminder for Amy (now aged one), settling her in gradually so she could develop a close relationship with her carer and not chopping and changing. In the event my high ideals were shattered. Everything went well at first: Amy's first minder lasted two months, but then she became ill and had to give up.

A very unsettling month followed, two childminders let us down after only a few days. Amy ended up coming to work with me for a few days when I was unable to work at home. Fortunately my colleagues were very understanding - without their support I would probably have given up and they enjoyed the novelty of having a baby in the office. However, found mixing motherhood with business distracting and embarrassing - I kept imagining people muttering about bringing children into the office.

During that month I must have seen just about every available childminder on the local social services' books. The social worker was helpful and must have been as relieved as me when I eventually found Glynis, who has now looked after Amy for five months. Though

Glynis lives a bit further away and is a bit more expensive than the previous minders, she is absolutely worth it. I often think Amy has a better time now than she would do at home: she has a nice garden to play in and ready-made friends in the form of Glynis' two sons (both at school) and another minded child. (Glynis takes Amy to a weekly childminders' group and on outings, such as picnics.)

My key to surviving as a working mum, now I have a reliable childminder, is having a routine. Organisation doesn't come easily to me, but now our family has a weekday system things more or less run smoothly. Paul gets Amy up and dressed each morning while I prepare and give her breakfast. In the evening Paul gives Amy her tea, we play for an hour and then it's her bathtime and bed by 7.30pm. I never do any housework during the week apart from washing up and clearing away toys each evening. Now I have come to terms with the fact that I'm not a superwoman and I can't fit in everything I should do, I can enjoy my job during the day and Amy's and Paul's company the rest of the time.

Childminder or Nanny?

Katherine

When I had Louise, my second daughter, my childminder - Janet - said that she could take her only if it were for term times only. Her reasons were perfectly understandable - she had two daughters of 5 and 8 and she didn't relish the prospect of looking after four children, including the baby, during the holidays. After a lot of thought we decided to try and find someone else to look after the children during the holidays rather than make the switch to a nanny all year round. Victoria, our elder daughter, had been with Janet for two years and loved her (and her daughters) so we were loath to break the arrangement. Also Victoria was conveniently going to the nursery class of the same school that Janet's children attended.

I fairly soon realised that my best bet was to find a teacher to share a nanny with and just after Christmas I found one. we jointly put an advertisement in The Lady for a daily nanny to look after my children during the holidays and theirs during term time - and received two replies (never try to recruit a nanny in January!). Fortunately one of them was (and is) excellent so we offered her the job. She has been a great success and I know that she has enjoyed the variety offered by the share arrangement.

I am now in a position to compare the relative merits of childminders and nannies and I have to say that for me the childminder wins hands down. What I have come to appreciate is the sheer lack of organisation involved when employing a childminder. You don't have to think about:

(a) whether your own house is vaguely tidy (your nanny may want to invite someone round so it's unfair to leave it a tip);

(b) if there's enough food in the house for the children's and nanny's lunch plus juice all day, etc;

(c) whether you ought to be discovering other nannies so that she can establish a network (childminder - who typically lives locally and has children of her own - will have her own friends and know her way round).

With a childminder you simply deliver the children and that's that. With a nanny the children found it more difficult to say goodbye as I left them in the morning than when I handed them over to Janet - for them while I was saying goodbye she was saying hello.

The only disadvantage of a childminder that everyone quotes is that you have to get yourself and the children up, washed, dressed, breakfasted and out every morning, summer and winter, but frankly I've never found this a problem. We get up at 7.45, get downstairs for breakfast by 8.15 and leave the house at 8.35. It was only a hassle when Victoria, aged 2, insisted on dressing herself - very slowly!

Oh, au pair

Susan

We have had ten au pairs in seven years with only one and a half unhappy experiences. I started working three days a week when Katie was a year old; she had a part-time place at a wonderful community nursery. However, after a year or so my husband and I found the 'I brought her yesterday, so you collect her tomorrow' dealings increasingly fraught, what with both of us in media jobs and with the vagaries of commuting. The only option seemed to be an au pair. Michael was most concerned about our privacy. I was worried about having to manage 'a servant'. Also, we had to move house to have room for her; but we planned to have a second child and would have moved at some time. Having put out the word, an au pair fell into our laps, a friend of a friend's Danish au pair. By arrangement Dorte stayed only 4 months. I was glad, because I thought I could make mistakes and learn by them in time for a full-year au pair. I was so nervous for Dorte's first two days I had a tummy ache. How bossy to be? How kind? How much to tell her? When? I'm no paragon of housekeeping, how do I know what I want? Finally I talked sternly to myself: 'She's more nervous of you than you should be of her!'. I got over it, though I still get a little tense over breaking in a new girl.

I thought out my house and my week and made a rough plan of how to use the au pair's 30 hours. In fact I have stapled together an 'Au Pair's Book of the Week' with chores and duties, a page per day. By advance arrangement I always say I want to spread their time into 6 hours over 5 days, with weekends entirely free, except for occasional weekend baby-sitting. With Alexander on the scene (he's now 2, Katie is nine and a half) I arrange and pay for more time. At 7 months he started at the community nursery 5 mornings a week, and gradually I have worked up to the au pair collecting and caring for him three days a week till 6pm. I work from home, so I encourage the au pair to take him to the park or One O'Clock Club, or else I just stay hidden in my office.

My au pairs do housework (hoover and dust and simple mopping). I figure about 2 hours a day for housework and 4 for childcare, keeping flexible about swapping days around or giving her free time if I have had to overuse her. I teach her simple meals for the children and usually she eats with them at around 6; Michael and I eat at around 9. We ALWAYS book her in advance for baby-sitting, so that she is free to make her own outside plans. Every au pair has dropped out of English classes. For one thing, we always have Danes and most speak English well. For another they have just finished years of school and are about to go back to more education, so they usually decide they want a year off. However, we encourage classes or some sort of structured outside activity (aerobics, volleyball) so they don't just loll about in their free time. We try to introduce them to other au pairs in our area and encourage a good social life. Most are keen NOT to be too involved in family life - remember when YOU were 18? I have learned new things - about my own ideas on housework, about personalities, about being a boss - from each au pair. Some have been particular favourites with Katie, and Alexander seems to adjust well to the changes. Oh, yes, the one and a half unhappy experiences: an au pair who transferred her difficulties with her mother to me (we parted after half a year); and a £200 leap in our quarterly phone bill, received after the departure of an otherwise pleasant girl. (We have a phone meter now.) I like to have a week between au pairs. It's nice to be a family by ourselves. And by the end of the week I realise how much I need an au pair!

On to School

Jackie

As my eldest daughter was approaching school age I started to panic! What was I going to do with her after school and during the school holidays? (As she was attending a day nursery which opened from 8.00 in the morning till 6.00pm daily except bank holidays, I had been able to continue with my work.)

Many thoughts came to mind such as, will I have to change my working hours and work part-time, or give up my work altogether? I approached my employers who were sympathetic but they were unable to change my working hours. After discussing my dilemma with some friends they suggested that I contact Social Services to see if they could help.

I contacted Social Services and they gave me the names and telephone numbers of a few childminders who might be able to help out and the number of a latchkey project. I didn't like the sound of the latchkey, I think it was the term 'latchkey' - which to me was very negative. I went to see the childminders all of which would have helped but they were too expensive for me.

I decided to visit the latchkey project and see what they were offering. It turned out that they not only collected the children from school but they also ran holiday playschemes covering all the school holidays. They provided various indoor and outdoor activities and as they picked up from two schools, the children were able to mix and meet other children in their peer groups that attended the other local schools. The latchkey, which is partly subsidised by the local authority, was only charging half the price of a local minder and was good value for what they were offering.

My daughter has always enjoyed going to the latchkey and to the playschemes: she is now 10 years old and very well established in the project. I now have another daughter who will also be starting there in September and can't wait. I have also become more involved in the project - first of all, servicing on the Management Committee, then as Vice Chair, and now as Joint Chair.

Without the project I might have had to give up my work and studies. I shall be ever grateful for the service that they provide and also for giving me the peace of mind that my children will be well taken care of after school and during the school holidays.

If only all local authorities provided for these projects - many more people would be able to work - but because of the lack of this facility in some areas parents are unable to do so.

Out of School Scheme

Ali

I've worked mostly on and sometimes off since Joshua was 6 months old. For four years I was a single mum and now that Josh is 10 things are definitely easier. No dressing, feeding and pushing prams round to the childminders at the crack of dawn.

I've had childminders, friendly neighbours, nurseries and now he goes to an after hours scheme at his school which I was very lucky to find at just the right time. It opened when the nursery that Josh attended decided to stop catering for older children and without it I have no doubt I would have given up working.

The good points: Josh adores the two teachers who run it and gets on well with all the other children. There are plenty of toys and games to keep them occupied, a television which to my relief isn't often used and a quiet corner. They have biscuits and a drink to keep them going until they get home.

As Josh is an only child I'm sure he enjoys the other children's company and the staff really seem to participate which I know from experience isn't always the case. As the scheme is in the school grounds I don't have to worry about how and who will take him.

The bad points: The scheme runs from 3.15 to 6pm (it used to be 5.30). This doesn't leave us enough time to pick him up so he is let in to our home (which is nearby) by a member of staff when they shut. He is on his own for a quarter of an hour and although Josh is particularly sensible for his age it does leave us anxious (he has people to go to or ring in an emergency). I have only heard of a handful of places with realistic opening hours. After all, most people finish work at 5.30 and travelling takes time. The only other option is a childminder or nanny which can be very much trial and error and is pricey.

Now the scheme is running at full capacity I think sometimes Josh feels a little overwhelmed at times as it can get very crowded. He has his moments when he would like me there at the school gates every day but if I gave up work tomorrow I am sure he would get bored quite quickly and I know I would.

Josh is quick-witted and full of confidence and always willing to 'have a go'. I am certain that if his upbringing hadn't been a little chaotic he wouldn't be as outgoing and at ease with new situations as he is.

Workplace Nursery

Gill

My little boy, Nicholas, was 2 years old last February.

When my maternity leave was over I asked to return to work part-time instead of full-time. The request was approved by the Council's Chief Executive.

Until the creche at Amersham Pool was opened I had to rely on the generosity of relatives and friends for looking after Nicholas while I was at work. Occasionally this led to problems if, for instance, my mother had an appointment at the hospital clinic and other relations had their own arrangements.

The creche opened in January 1991 and, for the first two weeks, Nicholas was the only child there. Gradually, other children started there.

It has been very helpful to me to know that Nicholas is under the supervision of trained staff if anything should occur; that he is subject to some discipline; and by being with other children on a regular basis he is learning the lessons of give and take and general behaviour. However well meaning grandparents and other relatives may be they cannot provide the same instruction.

For me the peace of mind means I can concentrate on my work without worrying, while I am still nearby if anything serious occurs and the creche staff need to contact me.

Altogether, being able to be at creche is really beneficial for both of us and will, I am sure, help Nicholas a great deal when playgroup or school days arrive.

Support at work

Jacqui

Whilst I was expecting my first child I learned that my company was planning to set up a Childminding Network followed by a workplace nursery.

This alleviated the great worry of how and where to find childcare when I eventually returned to work. In addition, myself and all prospective users of the childcare facilities, were actively encouraged to participate in determining the scheme's requirements. This made me a part of the decision-making process and ensured that the resultant facilities met my major needs and were familiar to me.

Whilst away on maternity leave my employers 'kept in touch' by:

- sending me copies of the monthly company-wide briefing magazine plus any significant bulletins;

- inviting me to attend any training/departmental meetings (at the Company's expense).

All this made my eventual return so much easier as I still felt 'part of things'.

My son (14 months old) is cared for by a registered childminder in my home village who is a member of my employer's Childminding Network.

The Network was set up by 'Childminding in Business!' and is administered by a coordinator (who is a childcare expert and well able to give very sensible advice to new parents like myself!). The Network has a Quality Charter detailing the standards of care expected, and guidelines to parents. The coordinator ensures that all childminders meet the standards required as well as arranging many training sessions, eg first-aid for children, constructive play, etc.

The network provides great benefits for both the childminder and the parents:

- assisting in locating, interviewing and setting up minding arrangements;
- regular follow-up visits (reassuring for the parents as well as helping the childminder to feel part of a team);
- provision of suitable 'stand by' minders for sickness/holiday/emergency cover;
- regular social and educational events to bring minders and the minded children together (a recent event was a Teddy Bears' picnic at a large country park);
- free equipment loan and toy library schemes (available to both childminders and parents).

From next autumn we will also have the option of a day-care workplace nursery. This will accommodate 40 children (six months until school age) each working day from 8.00am to 6.00pm.

The whole process of returning to work has been very smooth. Not only was I able to work the hours that I wanted but I was supported throughout this by the Childminding Network Coordinator and my employers, both of whom took the trouble to determine what I wanted and tried their hardest to accommodate my needs. I have now been able to resume my professional career on a part-time basis whilst feeling secure that my son is being well cared for (and his situation is being continually monitored) - I really do feel that I can 'have my cake and can eat it!'.

A Single Mother

Mary

Sarah was born in March of my final year at college. Finding work was difficult but necessary both financially and because I felt that I wanted to use my training. My first job was part-time. I started in September and after many 'phone calls to registered childminders I contacted one who would take a 6-month old baby. The week she was due to start the childminder let me down, but introduced me to a woman who was just starting to mind children. She was not registered, but I didn't have much choice. The fee was a third of what I earned and the arrangement was not ideal.

The following January I started to work full-time in the health service, but I didn't feel that the childminder was suitable on a full-time basis. There was a work creche, but places were limited, and it was difficult to get to and from, not being near where I work. By this time I had separated from Sarah's father and was living with my mother. She offered to look after Sarah until I found another childminder. I had put Sarah's name down at all the local nurseries when she was 3 months old, but I was advised that places were in great demand and that the waiting lists were long. It was a difficult time. We managed to get some part-time help but it was expensive and not a long-term option. Eventually I found another childminder, but after two weeks Sarah did not settle and we agreed to terminate the arrangement. Sarah was 15 months old. I felt very anxious about finding someone to look after her. I phoned the Under-5s officer for the area and explained my concern about the childminding situation. I asked her if there was any chance of getting a nursery place, given that I had a job and didn't want to give up working. Her response was very negative and I got the impression that unless my child was at risk there was nothing she could do. I went to a private nursery that had recently opened. Sarah could have started straight away but the fees were too high for me. I had been through the list of registered childminders and I was getting desperate. I phoned the Under-5s officer again and expressed my disgust at the lack of childcare provision in the area. She told me I was lucky to live in an area that catered so well for childcare. However, she did give me the name of a childminder who lived out of the area. I contacted her, and Sarah and I went to see her. She was wonderful, had two daughters and Sarah liked it there.

She started with the new childminder when she was 17 months old. It was a long day for her, as I had to drop her off at 8.10am and couldn't pick her up until 5.30pm. She was happy there, and life became easier. After a year a place became available at a community nursery. Sarah was two and a half. I decided to accept the place as it offered many opportunities for learning, had children of Sarah's own age, had a safe and spacious play area and was close to home.

Looking back, I had to rely on the support of family and friends. In many ways it would have been easier to stay at home, but that would have involved support from state welfare. After all, I had a job.

One more point is the amount of time that I had to take off work when either Sarah or the childminder was sick. Even at nursery there have been times when I have had to take time off at short notice due to staff shortages or other problems. I have been lucky to have an understanding boss.

Sarah is due to start school (part-time) in September when she is three and a half. She has a place from 9 - 11.30 but I work from 9 - 5. I think that difficulties in childcare are just beginning a new phase, as I haven't the faintest idea what arrangements to make. Even when she starts full-time at school there will be the school holidays. Any ideas?

Fathers do their part too

Peter

When I explain to people that I care for our two children for a substantial part of the time, the reactions are somewhat varied: from sheer astonishment (mainly from women) to absolute horror (mainly from men). To my mind, there is nothing taboo about fathers looking after children. it seems quite normal that Mums and Dads play an equal role.

We have two children: Sandy, aged five, and Iona, one. My wife, Isobel, is a statistician in the Office of Population Censuses and Surveys and has to commute to London. I am Head of Mathematics in a secondary school and do much of the administrative work like drawing up a timetable. During the school holidays, I take charge of all the childcare during the day and when I have to go into school, it is easy to take the children with me. During term time, a childminder looks after the children during the day and fortunately, with Isobel being able to work 'flexitime', she can take most Tuesdays off. We have been lucky in that we have had the same childminder ever since we have needed one.

A typical day in term time starts soon after 6.00am. Contrary to what most people imagine mornings to be like in a household, our starts to the day are very relaxed affairs. I have time to cook and eat a full

English breakfast, clear up and wash up afterwards, and assist with feeding the children if needed. I normally leave the house at around 7.30am which enables me to put in a good hour's work at school before the day begins. Isobel takes the children to the childminders, drops Iona off and accompanies Sandy to Nursery School, before catching her train into London. My part comes at the other end of the day when I leave school in time to pick up the children at 5.00pm. I then feed, bath and put them to bed. With the children settled down by about 7.30pm, I then prepare the evening meal in time for Isobel's return.

During the holidays, I look after the children all day. The days, I find, are not difficult to fill. During the summer months, we visit the local swimming pool practically every day. We also have a large garden where the children are quite happy to play with each other or amuse themselves for long periods while I tend to the plants. When the weather is not so good, we go out quite often. Rail travel is enjoyed by all three of us and is not expensive with a Family Railcard. We have been as far afield as Lincoln, Southend and the South Coast in a day's travel.

I am often asked how I cope with looking after two small children. While it can be quite hard work on occasions, I would not describe it as difficult and I gain immense pleasure from it. When it comes to nappy changing time, and we are away from home, being a male can provide a problem as baby changing facilities are often in the ladies' toilets. On one cold February day, I needed to change Sandy in the middle of Liverpool. I could hardly change him on some park bench, so I searched for a suitable room in a large department store. As this was in the ladies' toilets, my request had to go to the manageress who kindly cleared the area so that I could gain access. I received some very strange looks from women waiting to go in when I emerged! On another occasion, I had to take Sandy to hospital one Sunday after he trapped his fingers when we were on a day out. I had Iona with me as well and the doctor who saw us simply could not believe that I was on my own with two small children! He asked as to the whereabouts of Isobel three times - and even then I do not think that he was convinced! The fact that I had left Mum at home so that she could have a few hours peace and quiet just seemed to be beyond comprehension!

I find that the keys to successful minding of our two children lie in being well organised and adhering to a reasonable routine. I also refuse to allow myself to become wound up over an issue, in that I always assume a relaxed attitude. While it is necessary to be firm,

I tend not to worry about the little things. After all, does it really matter if Sandy wants a different cup for his drink? Who is going to worry if, when I am just about to put Iona to bed, I notice that her pyjama top is on back to front? Not troubling about trifles is, I am sure, a good antidote to any stresses and strains which looking after children may present!

It's up to Dad

Tom

When Stephanie was born two years ago it seemed obvious that Janene would return to work, as she earned more money. Her work is career oriented - she is a computer graphics designer - and it would have hurt her career to drop out. I'm a musician. A lot of my work is not paid, so I work flexible days doing French polishing to pay for Stephanie's childcare. It's up to me to arrange where Stephanie is in the day so Janene can concentrate on her job. For the first six months I took care of Stephanie. Then I tried childminders but I had to commit to the times and I needed more flexibility. At six months I put Stephanie's name on a nursery waiting list for a part-time place which came through when she was a year old - I pay for a full week's afternoon places, but I usually only use it three times a week. My mum has her own business, but on days when I do the French polishing she takes Stephanie in the mornings and then brings her to nursery, and I collect Steph at the end of the day. When I have a gig Mum collects her and then I collect Stephanie from her house at night. It's a lot of juggling around but she seems to be happy enough when she wakes up at home in the morning. Occasionally she stays at Mum's the whole night. Soon Stephanie will start three full days a week at the nursery. I'm glad because it will take the burden off my Mum. Throughout my various childminding stages she's helped so much and I feel guilty about it.

In the week Janene gets up and goes. She works really long hours. I have Stephanie in the mornings; I sort out domestic things, do something with her. When I have a gig that night there's the madness of loading up a van with musical gear and with Stephanie. It's tricky, especially when the lift is broken. I'm a total parent in the mornings, but sometimes I feel I'm acting a bit. I'm a little paranoid about other people's reactions to me, though I'm getting used to it now. At mother and toddler groups I'm the only bloke there and all the mums go off and have a social scene for themselves. I'm caught with Steph and all the other kids as well, climbing all over me, jumping off the slide. There's a barrier - do they think I'm a creep? Or maybe it's because I'm a young parent. Once I phoned up a mum and suggested I bring Stephanie around to play. It was almost like I asked her out to dinner - weird - put me off doing that again! I do meet other blokes at the swings, but when it was Steph and me all the time isolation was a problem.

I have a great feeling of relief when I drop Stephanie off at nursery: this is my time, I've got to make use of it. But even on days when I can work properly I get taken over by the parental thing. Half an hour before the nursery closes I have to say 'Sorry, I've got to go'. I feel guilty about so many things. Guilty about my mother, guilty about my work mates. I worry that I'm not 'girlie' enough with Stephanie. Everything you do is not done quite properly. You've got to learn to just switch into one or the other.

Working at home

Ros

I'd always imagined (pre-babies) that this was the perfect solution: go freelance and work at home and look after my own children as well. With a tiny baby who sleeps a lot it still seems feasible (that is assuming you still feel like work at that stage. I had to mark some exams, which is how I found out). But a toddler is a different matter.

My job is very flexible, I can work at the college or at home, I do prefer home as it's warmer, I'm less disturbed by students, I save time and money on travelling and I can see my family more. But it has taken a long time to learn how to do it. I think it helps to have somewhere to shut yourself away as far from the noise as possible. You will also need a great deal of self-discipline.

(a) Division of responsibility. If you are paying someone to look after your child then let her do it and don't interfere. This must sound obvious but it is very easy to appear in the kitchen mid-morning and find a crying child and assume that things are out of control when in fact they are not. If you can, sort this out at the beginning before resentment builds up. Have a rule if necessary - in our house requests for food and drink and other decisions are supposed to be referred to Lesley while she's on duty.

(b) Try not to 'be around' too much. For very small children out of sight is out of mind, but even older ones immediately want a cuddle or a book read or just your continuing presence once you appear. If necessary take an electrical kettle, thermos, sandwich lunch, telephone extension into your work room so you minimise appearances. This also means that if you go in and out of the house you may need to sneak out somehow or you end up with snivelling toddlers on the doorstep even if you are only going for half an hour. (Of course, an advantage is that you can often take them along which you wouldn't have been able to do at the office.)

(c) Keep them out of your work space. This applies more to older (3+?) children. Difficult without a fuss. Eventually it can become a rule-to-be-obeyed, but otherwise you need tact. I have some tedious games (cutting up scrap paper, sorting out my buttons) and usually boredom sets in, but at times you just have to resort to physical removal, trying to harden your heart.

(d) Trust whoever is looking after them. Don't rush out every time you hear screams, give them a chance. This goes with (a). It's not fair to your employee if she feels you are constantly listening out and probably criticising her; in fact many trained nannies are very reluctant to accept jobs where they will have parents in the house all day.

She's leaving home

Joan

My heart sank! After the agreed year our first nanny was leaving. What will my one year old feel? How will I cope? I had to move fast, as, despite good notice, there was not a lot of time to compose an ad, get it into the magazines etc. I arranged a 'handover' week to enable my baby to get used to Number 2 while Number 1 was still around. In the early weeks with the new nanny I'd rush home from work earlier than usual to spend longer with my child.

He accepted the change remarkably well. He happily waved me goodbye in the morning and seemed his usual self in the evenings. He started waking in the night - unusual for him - for a month or so, and this I took as a sign of stress. His new nanny found him to be happy and easy going in the day, though she said he was 'aloof' at first.

Since then I've realised nannies are a mobile breed. They tend to be young, and move on for all the usual reasons - to join boyfriends, to get a flat on their own, to leave nannying or to travel. I don't take their leaving personally as I know I am a good and fair employer. In the beginning I had fantasies of finding a nanny who would stay many years and become an old, trusted friend of the family. While such nannies do exist, they are rare and tend to be older than the average. Our first, and second, nanny stayed for a year, our third for two years, and we are now on our fourth. I make it clear when I interview that I expect a minimum commitment of a year. The three nannies who have left have honoured this, and have always arranged their leaving to suit us.

Our children, and those of our friends, do seem amazingly adaptable, accepting changes of nannies well. There seem to be fewer problems with a child under one as he/she is relatively open with strangers. At ages 1 and 2 it is more difficult. Both my children formed a very close, loving relationship with the respective nannies who cared for them when they were aged 1 - 2. Those feelings were not transferred to the next nanny and have not been repeated. From 3 on they can understand more, and are able to grasp that mummy and daddy are permanent fixtures (hopefully), while their nanny is not. Each new nanny, with her own blend of strengths and weaknesses, has made a contribution to our family. All in all, the changes seem to bother the adults more than the children.

Maternity leave - the second time

Sue

If you can afford it, and intend to work again, it makes sense to continue employing your childcarer while you are on your second maternity leave. Your first child has continuity of care - with someone with more energy than you have; your childcarer has a stable income; your second child will know it's carer from birth; you get more time to yourself before the baby arrives and more time with the new baby after it's birth; your return to work is less traumatic for all concerned. You may also be able to call on your carer to look after your first child while you are in labour and in the immediate post-parturition days.

However, don't expect your first child to fit in with your concept of maternity leave. I had visions of days and days stretching ahead doing things which I never had sufficient time or energy to do whilst working: sorting out the new baby's things; shopping out of peak time; stocking up the freezer for those bleak days (weeks) immediately after the birth; sunbathing in peace; redecorating the house; visiting friends or cinemas unencumbered; or just sleeping; plus of course spending more time with my first child doing things that mothers-at-home can do (making play-dough, going to gym club and dancing sessions, picnics, watching Playschool).

However, my son (nearly 3) had very different ideas. To his way of thinking, when I was at home I should give him my undivided attention. He was, after all, used to this state of affairs during my normal working life, and couldn't understand why all of a sudden I was expecting him to stay with his nanny when I was physically in the house.

He would follow me around all day, clinging to my knees, exhibiting classic pre-birth sibling anxiety symptoms. It became impossible to get him to leave the house without me, even though it was to do enjoyable activities such as swimming, picnics or visiting friends. I would spend time doing the most boring things such as sleeping or sorting out clothes, to convince him that life with Joanne was far more exciting. It was therefore a very difficult time for all of us: for Joanne who was trying to do her job properly; for Marcus who needed reassurance; and for me who needed peace of mind and body. I began to feel that I would have had more rest at work. So very soon I capitulated and spent more time with Marcus and Joanne, only following my own pursuits when I was allowed.

When the baby arrived, Marcus was suddenly less clingy and anxious - presumably the impending event had happened, and was no longer an unknown threat. He was more relaxed, more prepared to spend time with Joanne and to leave me with the new baby. We soon settled into a routine of me spending the morning with Guy, and in the afternoon we would all do something together. While I was therefore able to spend more time alone with my new baby than most mothers could, most of my maternity leave ambitions remained unfulfilled. I have now successfully returned to work for the second time.

From a nanny's point of view

Elaine

A nanny can be seen as a substitute mother who, in the temporary absence of the actual mother, tries to ensure a degree of stability for the children. A dedicated nanny will treat your children as she would her own and will be as concerned for their welfare as you are.

Some mothers worry and get upset over not seeing or noticing a first attempt, first words or first unsupported steps in her child's progress. The fact, though, that your child is progressing and is happy and confident with his or her nanny should take away some misgivings, and as there are so many things a child has to learn, you can guarantee to be there often at 'first attempt'.

Do try and agree on what to expect of your child as this will help your nanny. Try not to feel guilty about insisting that your child does as he or she has been asked, just to make up for time you have been away. It is less confusing for your child and less frustrating for the nanny if you are consistent on this, and it will help your child not to play one person's ideas against the other - something young children are remarkably skilled at!

Another aspect of having a nanny that worries a 'working mother to be' is the relationship, between her child and the nanny. The closer the relationship, the better. Do not be upset if your son (or daughter) says "Mummy go to work now" as soon as the nanny appears, and promptly waves you goodbye. All this means is that he has accepted the situation (though not necessarily understanding it), knows he will be seeing you later on and is looking forward to the tea parties, swimming outings and swing visits that usually make up the day. On the other hand, if he is unhappy when you leave, you can be assured that as soon as he hears the door shut, he will immediately change his 'tune' - literally - and with the help of his nanny, look forward to his next activity.

I can assure you that your child's love for his nanny will not detract from his love for you or anybody else in the family. It is a different sort of love - quite strong simply because of time and total commitment involved. Do not deny them this friendship as your nanny works hard trying to keep a balanced life for your child. She often has to act on your behalf, when disciplining, or dealing with an accident, deciding which method you would prefer.

When you come home at the end of your child's day and your work-day, this is the time when emotions are running high. You are probably tired and maybe feeling unsure having left your child all day and all you want to do for a few minutes is collect your thoughts and energy before tackling your home environment, but unless your child is out or asleep the likelihood of this happening is pretty remote. The reaction on seeing mother at the end of the day can be upsetting for everybody concerned. A child may appear as though she has been unhappy all day. On the contrary, it is usually the opposite as the mother can observe if she can creep in without anyone noticing.

The mother feels she must comfort her crying child and give in to demands which are often asked for by screams, otherwise she feels she is letting him down again. To help everyone's feelings, it is best if the mother can tell her child that she will not put up with the screams and help the child to calm down. A very good way is to read a tried and trusted book.

A nanny likes to feel needed and appreciated, but not taken advantage of. Do try and keep her working conditions as reasonable as possible. You might not mind, or notice, your knickers floating round the living room, or that the sink and rubbish bin are overflowing with crockery and rubbish respectively, but as she is going to be spending several hours (if not all day in bad wether) in the house and possibly entertaining, she may not be too happy about living in the mess or clearing it up. Do think of your house as her workplace and try to leave it for her as you would wish to find your workplace - basically organised. Another area where nannies often feel put upon is the routine of keeping the child's clothes and toys in order. It would help the nanny to enjoy her job if, when the parents are 'on duty', they would take care of the children's gear. The nanny tries to keep the house free of scattered toys, and tidies up at the end of her day and gets the child to help. It is very upsetting to arrive the next day to find the bedroom looking as though a tornado has hit it. Most nannies want to help you and your family to survive a busy day, but if too many annoying obstacles are put (or left!) in her path, you will find yourself losing nanny or having a frustrated or unhappy person in charge of your child. A lot of nannies are too shy or unsure how to approach you with any disagreements or misunderstandings in their duties.

Whether it is necessary to have a trained nanny or not is a worry to some families. A trained person has proven that she has had an education and has stayed the distance on a two year course but, as an untrained nanny myself, I feel that the main quality a nanny needs to have is experience of caring for children. A girl who has younger brothers and sisters, or nieces and nephews, has a good idea on how children act in circumstances such as crossing the road, climbing up and down stairs, on and off beds and similar. Common sense and interest in and love for children are totally necessary.

Whoever you choose, she will do her best in the right conditions, and your child should benefit by learning to mix with others outside the family and will look forward to bath-time with you around (if that's possible) and, of course, your precious weekends together.

USEFUL ADDRESSES

British Activity Holiday Association
Orchard Cottage, 22 Green Lane, Hersham, Walton on Thames,
Surrey KT12 5HD 0932 252994
Promotes and regulates the standards of quality and safety of
holiday camps. Nearly 100 member. Consumer guide lists and
describes member organisations.

British Council
English Teaching Information Unit, 10 Spring Gardens, London
SW1A 2BN. 071 930 8466
For the (free) Arels Felco Guide to private language schools if
you have an au pair.

Childcare Vouchers Scheme
Luncheon Vouchers Limited, 50 Vauxhall Bridge Road, London
SW1V 2RS. 071 834 6666

Daycare Trust
Wesley House, 4 Wild Court, London WC2B 5AU. 071 405 5617
Provides information on good quality daycare and promotes
'Childcare Links' local childcare information services.

Equal Opportunities Commission
Overseas House, Quay Street, Manchester M3 3HN.
061 833 9244
Useful for statistical information on childcare as well as more
obvious equal opportunities work.

Gingerbread
33 Wellington Street, London WC2E 7BN. 071-240 0953
Supports single parents and their children through the provision
of advice on financial, legal and social problems. Some local
groups provide day care for working parents.

Home-Run
Active Information, 79 Black Lion Lane, London W6 9BG.
081 741 2440
Newsletter for people who work from home.

Kids' Clubs Network
279-281 Whitechapel Road, London E1 1BY. 071 247 3009
Promotes the development of provision of out of school and
holiday care for children up to 12 years old. Useful literature on
setting up local after school/play schemes.

The related **Out of School Childcare Consultancy Service** assists employers and organisations in setting up schemes.

National Childbirth Trust
Alexander House, Oldham Terrace, Acton, London W3 6NH. 081 992 8637
Promotes education for parenthood; campaigns for flexibility and choice in birth arragements; supports breastfeeding; counselling and postnatal support branches.

National Childcare Campaign/Daycare Trust
Produce very useful literature on childcare, including statistics, how to set up a community nursery and organising local childcare campaigns.

National Childminding Association
8 Masons Hill, Bromley, Kent BR2 9EX. 081-466 0200
Promotes and coordinates the interests of childminders and seeks to improve the quality of childcare provided by them by increasing the resources available to them and through the provision of training courses. Produces useful literature for both minders and parents thinking of choosing a childminder and has a consultancy for employers - **Childminding - In Business!**

National Council for One-Parent Families
255 Kentish Town Road, London NW5 2LX. 071 267 1361
Research and parliamentary lobbying to improve every aspect of life for one parent families. Supports provision of day care facilities for working parents.

New Ways to Work
309 Upper Street, London N1 2TY. 071 226 4026
Information on flexible working and job-sharing.

Nursery World
Child Care Classified Department, The Schoolhouse Workshop, 51 Calthorpe Street, London WC1X 0HH. 071 837 7224
Takes classified advertisements for nannies.

OwnBase
68 First Avenue, Bush Hill Park, Enfield, Middlesex EN1 1BN.
A network and newsletter for people who work from their homes.

Pre-School Playgroups Association
61-63 Kings Cross Road, London WC1X 9LL. 071 833 0991
Promotes public interest in play and the study of the needs and problems of under-5s and their parents.

Rights of Women
52-54 Featherstone Street, London EC1Y 8RT. 071 251 6577
Offers free legal advice, especially helpful in employment disputes.

The Home Office
Lunar House, Wellesley Road, Croydon CR9 2BY. 081 686 0688
For information on regulations for au pairs from outside the EC.

The Independent
40 City Road, London EC1Y 2BD. 071 253 1222
Takes classified advertisements for nannies.

The Lady
39-40 Bedford Street, London WC2E 9ER. 071 379 4717
Takes classified advertisements for nannies.

The Maternity Alliance
15 Brittania Street, London WC1X 9JP. 071 837 1265
Offers free advice on employment and maternity rights of pregnant women.

The Pepperell Unit
The Industrial Society, Robert Hyde House, 48 Bryanston Square, London W1H 7LN. 071 262 2401
Helps organisations make the best use of the skills and abilities of their women employees.

Women Returners' Network
8 John Adams Street, London WC2N 6EZ. 071 839 8188
Provide information on courses to update you in your field, self-assessment and career planning.

Working for Childcare
77 Holloway Road, London N7 8JZ. 071 700 0281
Promotes the development of workplace nurseries (and all work-related childcare) together with research and information on the subject. **Working for Childcare Limited** is an associated consultancy providing assistance to employers in setting up workplace childcare.

THE WORKING MOTHERS ASSOCIATION – PUBLICATIONS

THE WORKING PARENTS HANDBOOK

A practical guide to the alternatives in childcare from childminder to nanny to nursery to out-of-school schemes. Factors to consider in choosing childcare. How to find and interview carers, pay tax and National Insurance. Updated to include The Children Act 1989 and augmented by information on parents at work, including employers' 'family friendly' initiatives and flexible work patterns.

EMPLOYER'S GUIDE TO CHILDCARE

Written for managers and task-groups, this 132 page book examines the many ways employers can help working parents. Examples of workplace initiatives from over 80 employers in the UK include childcare benefits, workplace nurseries, career break schemes and job-sharing. Costs and benefits are assessed.

WMA MATERNITY PACK

A useful, comprehensive guide to help women get the best from their maternity leave. Includes The Working Parents Handbook and WMA Newsletter, list of local WMA support groups, and other material. For individuals or for companies who want to give packs as a cost-effective way to encourage women to return to work.

WMA RETURNERS HANDBOOK

Essential information to help women get started with planning a return to work, including when, plus careers advice and training courses. Also, looking for work, filling in application forms, interviews and childcare information. New for Spring 1994.

WMA NEWSLETTER

For working parents, this is a magazine style publication, full of news, information and personal experiences. Free with annual membership or may be purchased individually.

INFORMATION LEAFLETS

WMA: Who are we?
Why Your Company Should Belong (Corporate Membership)
Setting Up A Local Group
About WMA Workshops

CARER'S CONTRACT

Ready-made, incorporating all areas you should cover when employing nanny/mother's help. Blanks to fill in your own details. Free to members.

ONE-DAY SEMINARS

Including information pack plus lunch and refreshments. Open to individuals or to companies who wish to send employees. WMA can also run courses in-house for employers.

Taking Maternity Leave

Work and pregnancy (organising your time effectively, managing stress, understanding maternity benefits), relationships and self (relaxation, changes), planning after the birth (new emotions, deciding on childcare).

Back to Work

Being a working mother (managing the balance, dealing with fatigue, a five year plan), mixed feelings (separating from your child, finding your confidence, realising your ambitions), childcare (interviewing carers, settling your child).

WMA MEMBERSHIP FORM

Membership year runs for twelve months from 1st April to 31st March. However, applications received after January 31st will run until 31st March of the following year. The following fees apply until 31.3.94.

Individual Membership

I am applying for membership and enclose a cheque/P.O. for £12.50 for one year, or £33.00 for three years, which will entitle me to one copy of *The Working Parents Handbook* and a copy of each of the newsletters.

Name _____

Address _____

_____

Tel. No. _____ (Home) _____ (Work)

Please make cheques/P.O. payable to the
Working Mothers Association, 77 Holloway Road, London N7 8JZ

We should be grateful if you would complete the questionnaire below for our records:

1. Do you have any special areas of expertise which would be useful to us, eg journalist, auditor, publisher, etc?

_____

2. Do you have any special areas of interest, eg single parent, handicapped children, over-10s, twins?

_____

3. How did you find out about the Working Mothers Association?

_____

4. Individual Membership

    4.1 Type of work/occupation _____

    4.2 Full-time/part-time _____

    4.3 Number and ages of children _____

    4.4 Current childcare arragements _____

    4.5 Would you mind being contacted by other WMA members? Yes/No

    4.6 Do you belong to a local WMA group? Yes/No

        If yes, group name _____

        Address & tel. no. _____